Reading

for Christian Schools® 2-1

Bob Jones University Press, Greenville, South Carolina 29614

018655

Consultants

from the administration and faculty of Bob Jones University

Grace C. Collins, Ph.D., *Chairman, Department of Linguistics*
Walter G. Fremont, Ed.D., *Dean of the School of Education*
Melva M. Heintz, M.A., *Elementary Principal*
Janice A. Joss, M.A.T., *Graduate School of Education*
Betty Anne Rupp, M.A., *Professor of Reading, School of Education*
Philip D. Smith, Ed.D., *Provost*
Hazel M. Truman, M.A., *Project Director, University Press*

Curtis Brown, Ltd.: "This Tooth," by Lee Bennett Hopkins, reprinted by permission of Curtis Brown, Ltd. Copyright ©1970 by Lee Bennett Hopkins.

Creation Science Foundation, Ltd.: photographs, pp. 99-105.

Houghton Mifflin Company: Glossary material based on the lexical database of the *Children's Dictionary,* copyright ©1981 Houghton Mifflin Company. No part of this book may be reproduced or transmitted in any form or by any means, electronic or mechanical, including photocopying and recording, or by any information storage or retrieval system, except as may be expressly permitted by the 1976 Copyright Act or with prior written permission from both Houghton Mifflin Company and the Bob Jones University Press.

READING for Christian Schools® 2-1
Produced in cooperation with the Bob Jones University School of Education and Bob Jones Elementary School.

ISBN 0-89084-186-1

©1982 Bob Jones University Press
Greenville, South Carolina 29614

20 19 18 17 16 15 14 13 12 11

Contents

Days to Remember

Creatures Great and Small

Treasures

DAYS TO REMEMBER

Something Grand

Someone Grand

Don set his black Bible on the desk. "Mother," he said, "my Bible has a rip on the top. Will you help me fix it?"

Mother mended the rip. "There, that will do for now," she said. "I have something to tell you. Someone is coming to visit us."

"Who?" Don asked.

"Someone 'grand,' " she said.

"Is it Granddad?" Don asked.

"Yes, Granddad is coming. He will visit for six days," Mother said. She handed Don his Bible. "Run and get your jacket. We must pick up Dad at the shop."

Don left his Bible on the stand by his bed. He ran to get his jacket. "Am I quick?" he asked as he zipped it up.

Mother nodded. They left for Dad's shop. When they stopped, Don ran in to get Dad. He skipped to the back of the shop.

"Dad," Don yelled. "Granddad is coming to visit!"

Dad grinned at him from his desk. "I heard that too. Come on, Don," he said. Dad got up and locked the shop.

The Missing Bible

"Don, you must get up for school," Mother said.

"Is Granddad here?" he asked.

"Not yet," said Mother.

Don sat up. He dressed quickly. As he slipped on a sock, he looked at the stand by his bed. "That is funny," he said. "My Bible is missing."

Don finished dressing and went to look for his Bible.

"Mother, do you have my Bible?" Don asked.

"No, I do not have it," Mother said.

"I left it on the stand and now it is not there," Don said.

"Dad may have your Bible. He wants to mend it so that you cannot see the rip," Mother said.

Just then Dad came in. Someone was with him. "Look who is here," said Dad.

"Granddad!" Don said. He hugged Granddad. "Mother said someone grand was coming to visit."

A Bible for School

Granddad sat by Don. Dad asked the blessing. Mother handed Don his milk.

"My Bible is still missing," Don said sadly. "I must have a Bible for school."

"I see," Granddad said. He looked at
Dad. "May I give Don the gift I have for
him?"

Dad nodded. He handed a bag to Granddad. Granddad lifted a box from the bag.

"Here, Don. This is for you," he said.

Don lifted the lid of the box.

"Oh, Granddad, a Bible. A red Bible,"
Don said. He hugged Granddad.

Don held up the Bible. "D-o-n
H-o-p-k-i-n-s," he spelled. "Don Hopkins is
printed on the top. This is my Bible! It is
a grand gift, Granddad."

"There is something else in the bag," said
Dad. Granddad held up a black Bible.

"That is my missing Bible," said Don.

"Dad fixed the rip so that you cannot see it," said Mother.

Don said, "Now I have a black Bible for here and a red Bible for school."

The Big Fish
Let's Go!

"This is the last day of my visit," Grand-dad said. "Let's go fishing!"

"Maybe we will get the Big One today!" said Don.

Mother fixed a snack for Don and Granddad.

"Grab our fishing rods, Don," Granddad said. "I want to see that big fish in your pond."

Don ran to get the fishing rods. Off they went to the pond.

"Big One lives by that log in the pond,"
said Don. "Can you see him yet?"

"No, not yet," said Granddad.

They propped up their fishing rods.
Granddad sat on a rock. Don sat on the
grass.

Granddad tilted his hat.

"Did you have fun at school today?" he
asked.

"Yes," said Don. "And my red Bible is in my desk."

"I am glad that you can go to a Christian school, Don," said Granddad.

"Me too," said Don.

Just then Don heard a splash. He sat up.

"Is that Big One?" asked Granddad.

"Yes, look!" Don said.

Big One jumped. Splash! He fell back into the pond.

"There he is! What a big fish!" said Granddad.

Big One

Granddad and Don got their fishing rods. They sat still.

Splash! went Big One. Then the pond was still. "Where did he go?" asked Don.

"Maybe he went to the bottom of the pond," said Granddad.

Just then Don felt a tug on his fishing rod.

"Granddad, I have Big One!" he yelled.

The big fish jumped and jumped. The rod dipped and bent. It slipped in Don's hands. Don grabbed for the rod, but he slipped on the grass. The fishing rod fell into the pond.

Off swam the big fish.

Granddad helped Don up. Don looked at the pond. "My fishing rod is in the pond, and that big fish is back in the pond. I did not get him today."

Then Don grinned. "I am glad that I did not get him. I do not want to see him in a pan!"

"Yes," said Granddad. "Now he just may still be here when I come back to visit you. But we must go now."

Granddad got Don's fishing rod from the pond. Don and Granddad went back up the hill. They stopped at the top and looked back at the pond.

Splash! went Big One.

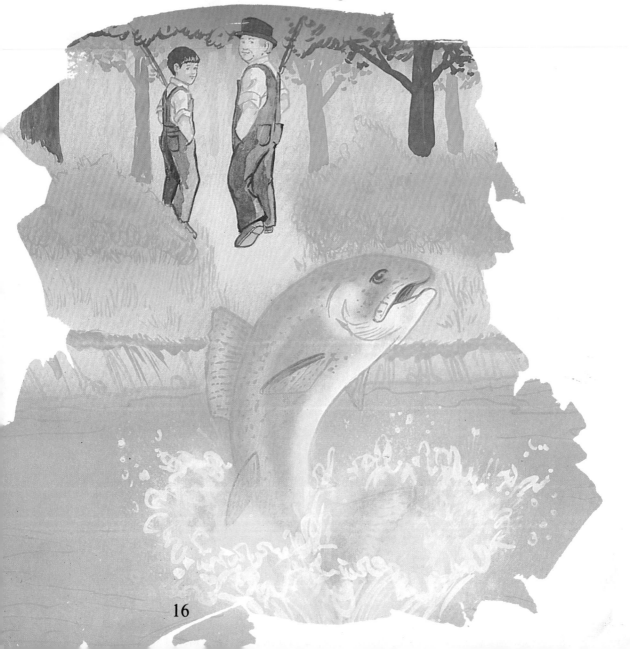

Samuel, God's Servant

(taken from I Samuel 2 & 3)

In the Tabernacle

One day Samuel's mother went with him to the tabernacle. "Now you will live in the tabernacle with Eli," she said. "You can serve God here."

Samuel asked, "Will you visit me?"

"Yes, I will visit you every spring," said his mother.

Samuel's mother hugged him and kissed him. Then she left him in the tabernacle with Eli.

"I am glad you have come, Samuel," said Eli. "I cannot do some of the jobs here. You will be a big help."

Samuel was happy in the tabernacle. He lit the lamps. He rubbed the brass cups with a rag. He ran here and there to get things for Eli.

Samuel was a servant of God.

Who Was Speaking?

Eli's sons did not serve God. They did not do what God said to do. But Eli did not punish his sons. He let them live in God's tabernacle.

God was not happy with Eli's sons. He was not happy with Eli. But God could see that Samuel wanted to serve Him. God could speak to Samuel.

One day after Samuel had finished his jobs, he went to bed. Suddenly, in the stillness, Samuel heard someone speak to him!

"Samuel! Samuel!" someone said.

Samuel jumped up from his bed and ran to Eli. "Here I am, Eli. Did you want me?"

Eli blinked and looked at Samuel. "I did not speak to you," Eli said. "Now go back to bed."

Samuel went back to bed. But he did not understand. "Someone was speaking to me," he said to himself. "Who was it?"

"Samuel!"

Samuel jumped up from his bed and ran back to Eli. "Here I am, Eli," he said. "You did want me."

"No, I did not want you," Eli said. "Go back to bed."

Samuel went back to bed. But he could not rest.

God's Servant

"Samuel!"

Samuel rushed back to Eli. "I heard you, Eli! I did hear you speak! You wanted me!"

Eli sat up on his bed. He did not tell Samuel to go back to bed. Eli said, "Samuel, maybe God was speaking to you. When you hear Him, say, 'Speak, Lord, for Your servant hears.' "

Back in bed, Samuel sat up and stretched. Everything was still until he heard someone speak.

"Samuel!"

Samuel's chin trembled. But he remembered to do what Eli had said to do. "Speak, for Your servant hears," he said.

God said, "Samuel, Eli's sons are wicked. Eli has not punished them. So I must punish Eli and his sons. They have not served Me."

The next day Eli said, "Samuel, what did God tell you?"

Samuel did not want to tell Eli what God had said. But he did tell him. Eli nodded. "The Lord will do what is best," he said.

God kept on speaking to Samuel when he was a lad and after he was a man. Samuel would tell everyone what God had said. He was the servant God wanted.

Someone My Age
Donna Wants a Friend

"May I go jump rope, Mother?" asked Ann.

Mother smiled. "Yes," she said.

"May I ride my bike?" asked Ken.

"Yes," said Mother.

Donna went to sit on the steps. Mother came to sit with her.

"Mother," Donna said, "Ann has a friend in Apartment 28. Ken has a friend in Apartment 32. But I do not have a friend here."

24

"You have friends at school," said Mother. "You can ask one of them to come home with you."

"That is not the same as having a friend who lives close to me," said Donna.

"Well," Mother said. "The Blakes are renting Apartment 48. I met them when they came to look at the apartment. They had someone your age with them. Maybe she will be your friend."

Donna looked up and smiled. Mother gave her a hug. "Now run and skate," she said.

Donna ran to get her skates. Mother helped her strap them on. Off Donna skated. She waved at Ann and her friend. They were skipping rope.

She skated past Ken and his friend. They were riding their bikes. Donna waved as they rode past her.

Someone Donna's Age

Donna skated back to her apartment. A van drove up to the apartments and stopped. Donna stopped to look. The van backed up to Apartment 48!

Donna skated a little closer. She could see a man and a lady taking in a table. She could see them taking in a desk. She could see them taking in lots of boxes. Then the man lifted a bike from the back of the van. Donna skated even closer to look. It was a bike just like hers!

The lady looked up. "Hello," she said. "I am Mrs. Blake. Who are you?"

"I am Donna Stevens," Donna said. "I am seven. Do you have someone my age?"

The lady smiled. "Yes, Kelly is inside the van. Come here, Kelly," she said.

Kelly jumped to the grass. She stopped and looked at Donna.

"Hello," said Donna.

Kelly just smiled. Then she went inside Apartment 48.

"Kelly is shy," said her mother. "Just give her more time. She would like to have a friend. Come back and visit us."

"I will," said Donna. She skated home.

One Step, Two Steps

When Donna got home, Mother was fixing dinner.

"Did you see someone your age?" asked Mother.

Donna dropped her skates in the box. "Yes," she said. "I spoke to her, but she did not speak to me."

"Did she hear you?" asked Mother.

"Yes," Donna said. "But she is shy."

"Why not try speaking to her every day? You can ask her to go with you to Sunday school," Mother said.

And that is what Donna did.

Every day she skated past Apartment 48. Every day she spoke to Kelly. "Would you like to go to Sunday school with me?" she would ask.

"No, thank you," Kelly would reply.

One day Kelly was sitting on her steps. She had some skates in her hand.

Donna stopped. "Can you skate?" she asked.

"Not yet," said Kelly.

"You just take one step, then two steps and slide," said Donna. "Let me help."

She strapped on Kelly's skates. Then Donna skated beside Kelly. Kelly wobbled from side to side. At last she stopped to rest.

"Do you still go to Sunday school?" asked Kelly.

"Yes," said Donna. "Will you go with me?"

"Mother said that I could go. Will you stop for me Sunday?" Kelly asked.

"Yes, I will," Donna smiled.

Donna hummed as she skated home. "Now I have a friend," Donna said. "I have a friend who is my age!"

Flying!

(based on historical research)

Wilbur Wright looked at the glider that he and Orville had just tested.

"Orville, we have made gliders that can ride on the wind," Wilbur said. "We have even made big gliders that we can ride in. But those gliders did not have motors. Now I think it is time for us to make an airplane that can fly with a motor and a propeller."

Orville agreed. For days and days the two men planned their airplane. Then they cut boards. They tied wires. They stretched cloth over the wings. They used chains from bikes to connect the gears.

In the winter the plane was finally finished and set to go. On a chilly day in 1903, the two men went to a little hill by the beach. Orville Wright got into the airplane. "Now give the motor a crank!" he said.

Wilbur cranked the motor. What a clatter they heard! "I hope it can fly!" Orville yelled. Wilbur just grinned back at him.

The little airplane glided on the beach. Then it began to rise into the air. Up, up, up it went.

Wilbur cheered. "We did it, Orville! We did it!" he yelled.

Orville could not hear him. He just heard the racket that the motor made. But when the plane landed a moment later, the two happy men hugged each other and slapped each other on the back.

"No one has ever used a motor to make an airplane fly," Orville exclaimed. "We finally did it!"

Little Bug's Trip

Little Bug Leaves Home

Little Bug bent over and looked at himself in the lake.

"I am quick. I am brave. I am clever. I am the best bug there is," he bragged.

His head tipped this way and that as he fixed his little red cap. His chest swelled until a button popped from his crisp red coat.

"It is time for me to leave home. I can take care of myself," Little Bug said.

Little Bug tilted his little bug cap, tied his little bug shoes, and buttoned the other two buttons on his little bug coat. Then he buzzed away.

He hummed happily to himself as he left. "I am quick. I am brave. I am clever. I am the best and that is that."

Little Bug landed on a rock. A duck was nearby.

"Quack, quack," he heard the duck say. She tilted her head and flapped her wings. "Come play with me and be my friend, Little Bug."

"Oh, ho!" Little Bug bragged to himself. "This duck would like to see what a fine bug I am."

He buzzed closer and perched on a red and yellow leaf.

"You are a *fat* bug!" quacked the duck, nodding her head. "I like fat bugs the best."

Little Bug tipped his little bug cap. He began to speak. But before he could say anything—snap! went the duck's yellow bill.

The duck got Little Bug's shoe.

A sudden breeze sent the red and yellow leaf flying. Now Little Bug was underneath the leaf. His little heart was going thump, thump!

Little Bug Hides

Little Bug peeked up from underneath the leaf. Now he could not see the duck anywhere.

"Oh, oh!" he said to himself. "That duck was quick!"

Little Bug wiggled from under the leaf. One of his two little bug shoes was missing. One more button from his little bug coat was missing. But his little bug cap was still perched on his head.

"I am not quick. But I am brave and I am clever," he said.

Little Bug puffed up his chest so big that the last button popped from his little bug coat.

Suddenly a black shadow fell over him. Little Bug heard a flap, flap. He looked up. A big black crow was flying closer and closer to him!

Little Bug could feel himself shaking. He was shaking from the top of his little bug head to the tips of his little bug toes.

He scampered back under the leaf. His little heart went thump, thump!

The black crow flapped his wings and went away. Little Bug's teeth stopped chattering. He buzzed away and landed on a rose.

Little Bug tapped the brim of his little red cap. He said, "I am not quick and I am not brave, but I am clever."

He buzzed nearer to the lake.

Little Bug Buzzes Home

"I see a frog," Little Bug said to himself. "I am more clever than he is."

"Is that a bug?" croaked the frog, hopping onto a lily pad. "Come closer, Little Bug. Give me a better look at you. I would like to see what a fine bug you are."

Little Bug perched on a stick closer to the frog.

But the frog said, "I have lived many years and cannot see well. Come closer still."

Little Bug buzzed to the end of the stick.

"I am a fine-looking bug, friend Frog," he said. But before he could say anything else—zap! went the old frog's tongue.

But the frog got just the little red cap.

Splash! Little Bug's last shoe fell into the lake. His open coat flapped as he buzzed quickly to a treetop.

"That frog was clever!" he said. "If he could see well, I would not be here!"

Little Bug hung his head. "I am not quick. I am not brave. I am not clever. I can see my side of the lake. I am going home."

And he did.

Missing Ribbons

Pat's Ponytail

Pat brushed her hair into a ponytail. She slipped a rubber band over the end. Then she skipped to the kitchen.

"Mother," she said. "I do not have any ribbons. May I get one to tie my ponytail?"

"Yes, I am going shopping today," Mother said. "Do you want me to wait until you come home from school?"

Pat nodded. "I do not need many, but I would like to pick my own ribbons," she said.

After school Pat and Mother drove to the store.

Pat looked at every ribbon in the store. At last she chose two red and two green ribbons. She paid the clerk and skipped to the car.

At home Pat ran up the steps. She wanted to try on her ribbons.

"Pat!" Mother said. "Please give me some help bringing in the bags from the car."

"Oh, I forgot them!" Pat exclaimed. She set her ribbons on the steps and went back to the car.

Pat sang as she helped her mother with
the bags. She heard the robin that lived in
the oak tree singing back. He hopped onto
the grass near the steps and cocked his
head in a friendly way.

At last the car was empty.

"Go try on your ribbons," Mother said.
"I would like to see them in your hair."

Pat skipped from the kitchen to the steps. But her ribbons were not there! Not even the robin was there. The steps were empty.

Pat looked in the car and under the car. The ribbons were still missing.

"Maybe they fell," she said to herself as she looked from the steps to the grass.

Green grass stretched from one side of the yard to the other, but no red or green ribbons lay hidden in it.

Clips for Pat

Mother helped Pat look for the ribbons. They looked under the steps and in the rose bed. They did not see the ribbons anywhere.

Just then they heard Dad driving up in the driveway. Mother and Pat waved from the porch.

"Hello!" Dad said. "What are you doing?"

"We are looking for my ribbons!" Pat said.

"Ribbons?" Dad asked. "If you have ribbons, do you need these?"

He held up a little bag from his pocket and handed it to Pat.

Pat could feel something hard in the bag. She tipped the bag. Some shiny clips fell into her hand.

"Oh, Dad!" Pat exclaimed. "Thank you!"

She reached up to give Dad a hug. Two silver clips were shaped like tiny robins. Pat clipped one on each side of her head.

"I am glad you have some clips. Now they will keep your hair away from your eyes!" Mother said.

"I will not stop looking for my ribbons yet," Pat said. "But I like these clips. Did you see them, Mother? They are tiny robins, just like the ones that live in the oak tree by my window."

Every morning Pat brushed her hair well to keep it from tangling. Then she wore her clips. Her friends at school liked them. But she still wanted her ribbons.

Ribbon Robbery

The weeks passed quickly. Many times Pat played in the yard after she got home from school. One day she heard some tiny peeps coming from the oak tree.

"The robins have a family now!" Pat said to Mother.

Mother went to the tree with Pat. She said, "If you look every day, you may see the baby robins when they begin to fly."

Pat checked the oak tree every morning. At last the day came. A baby robin hopped from the nest and fluttered to the grass. Pat sat still. The robin flapped its wings until it rose up to a low branch. It rested there, and Pat ran to tell Mother.

Before too many weeks passed, the baby robins had grown up. Many more weeks went by. Then one chilly morning, Pat did not see the robins.

"Good-bye, robins," Pat said to herself. "I will not see you until spring."

The leaves fell from the trees, and Pat helped her Dad rake. Sometimes she would rake up a big pile, then run and jump into it. Even her hair would have leaves stuck in it.

"Look, Pat!" Dad said. "The robins' nest must have blown off its branch."

Pat jumped up and skipped to the oak tree. The nest lay in the leaves.

Pat could see a tiny bit of green and a tiny bit of red on the nest.

"What is this?" she asked, picking it up.

"Oh, Dad," she cried. "My missing ribbons!"

"The robins must have woven them into their nest," Dad said.

"So, those robins were the ribbon robbers!" Pat said with a chuckle. "Well, at least my ribbons helped to make a good, snug bed for those baby robins."

Billy Sunday

A Baseball Player Gets Saved

The streetcar ran clicking and clacking on its rails. Ann sat by her dad, humming the tune they had sung at the tent meeting. "Daddy," she said at last, "I liked hearing Mr. Sunday preach. Did you ever see him play baseball?"

"Yes, Ann," Dad said, nodding his head. "I saw him play before he began preaching in tent meetings. Mr. Sunday ran like the wind when he played baseball. Because he could run so fast, he could catch more fly balls than any of the other players.

"Mr. Sunday helped his team, the White Stockings, win lots of games. One day he was walking with two of the men on his baseball team. They heard singing. It made Mr. Sunday think of his mother's singing. His friends went home, but Mr. Sunday stayed to listen.

"A man preached. He said that Christ had come to save sinners. Mr. Sunday left, but he did not forget what the preacher had said. One glad day, Mr. Sunday asked Christ to take away his sins and save him."

"He trusted Christ, just like I did today!" Ann exclaimed.

"Yes, Ann." Dad gave her a hug.

A Long Reach

Ann sat closer to Dad. She wanted to hear more. "What did Mr. Sunday do after he was saved?" she asked.

"Mr. Sunday kept playing baseball. One day his team played a big game. The game was really close. The best man on the other team was up to bat.

60

"The White Stockings waited for their pitcher to toss the ball. Just as he let it go, his leg slipped. The ball went where the batter wanted it. The batter hit that ball with a crack! It went flying across the ball park. Mr. Sunday began to run. Now was not the time to miss. He had to catch that ball or the game would be lost!

"Mr. Sunday ran as fast as he could. He wanted his team to win. He had to catch that ball.

" 'Lord,' he prayed, 'help me to catch that ball!' Mr. Sunday ran to the end of the ball park. His eyes never left that ball. He saw the ball starting to fall. He held up his mitt and jumped.

"The ball hit his mitt with a thump, but Mr. Sunday kept going. He tripped over a bench and fell under some horses. When he picked himself up, the ball was still in his mitt!

"Everyone yelled and yelled. Mr. Sunday's team had not lost! The White Stockings were the winners."

God's Preacher

"Why did Mr. Sunday stop playing baseball, Daddy?" Ann asked.

"God had a plan for Mr. Sunday, Ann," Daddy said, "just as He has a plan for you. God's plan for Mr. Sunday was for him to be a preacher. Mr. Sunday wanted to do what God wanted, but he liked playing baseball too.

"One day he said, 'I will quit playing baseball now if my team will let me go. I said I would play for them for three years. I cannot leave if they will not let me.'

"He asked his team if he could leave. They said, 'No, we need you. You said you would play. We cannot let you go.'

"God still wanted Mr. Sunday to be a preacher. Mr. Sunday kept praying. Many weeks went by. Then one day, the team said Mr. Sunday could quit.

"So Billy Sunday became a preacher for Christ."

The streetcar stopped near where they lived. Daddy and Ann got off, and the streetcar click-clacked away.

"Mother!" Ann called when they reached the steps. "We heard Mr. Sunday preach today in the tent meeting. He was a baseball player before he became a preacher. Daddy saw him play one time. And Mother, today at the tent meeting I asked Christ to save me!"

Mother gave Ann a kiss. "Good! I am glad," she said. "God has a plan for your life, Ann."

"Yes, just like He had a plan for Mr. Sunday," Ann said.

This Tooth

I jiggled it
    jaggled it
    jerked it.
I pushed
    and pulled
    and poked it.
But—

As soon as I stopped, and left it alone,
This tooth came out on its very own.

Lee Bennett Hopkins

Making Do

Cast:

Narrator

Two peddlers: Ben and Will

Farmer

Miller

Doctor

Part I

Narrator: Two peddlers walked along a dusty road. They carried packs on their backs. One stopped and dropped his pack on the road.

Will: I cannot go one step farther!

Ben: We cannot stop here. Look at the sky. A storm is coming.

Will: Oh, no! I am hot and I am tired and I am hungry. Now I am going to get wet too!

Ben: There is an empty barn. We can stay there until the storm is over.

Narrator: Will picked up his pack, and the two men ran to the barn. As they reached the empty barn, rain began to fall. The two peddlers dropped their packs into one of the empty stalls.

Will: Just look at that rain! We will
never get to the market!

Ben: The storm will not last long. We
will be on our way in the morning. At least we are not hot any
more.

Will: But I am still tired and hungry.

Ben: Let's see what we have left in our
packs. There may be something
we can make do for our supper!

Will: Make do! Make do! That is all
we ever do.

Narrator: Ben unpacked his pack. He flipped it bottom side up. One potato tumbled into the hay. Ben picked it up and wiped it off.

Will: What good is one potato?

Ben: Wait and see.

Narrator: There was an open shed on the back of the barn. Ben cleared a spot in it and made a fire. He filled a pot with rainwater. He set the pot on the fire. When the water was bubbling, Ben chopped up the potato and dropped it into the pot.

Will: Someone is coming!

Part II

Narrator: A farmer led his horse into the
barn. He held his horse still
when he saw the peddlers.

Farmer: Hello! You must be on your
way to market too.

Ben: Yes, come and stand by the fire.
I will lead your horse to a stall.
Then we will have something to
eat.

Farmer: Thank you.

Narrator: Ben led the farmer's horse to a stall. Will followed Ben.

Will: We have one potato. We cannot feed anyone else!

Ben: We will just have to make do.

Will: Making do! Making do!

Narrator: Will stalked back to sit by the fire.

Farmer: Mmm. That soup smells good! What is it?

Will: I think we will call it "making do" soup. We have it every day.

Farmer: What is in it?

Will: This time we had just one potato.

Farmer: That is all? Many things are good in soup. I have some beans on my cart. Could you use beans in your soup?

Will: Well, it will be better than soup with just one potato.

Narrator: The farmer went to get the beans. He came back with a big basket. The three men snapped the beans and dropped them into the black pot. The farmer stopped to stretch.

Farmer: I hear something.

Narrator: The three men looked up as a miller led his donkey into the barn.

Ben: Come and get dry. You can share our soup too.

Miller: Thank you. Soup is just fine on a day like this.

Farmer: Will calls it "making do" soup.

Miller: I like soup. My granny used to drop all the leftovers into the pot. What is in your soup?

Ben: We started with water, . . .

Will: and chopped in a potato, . . .

Farmer: and added some beans.

Miller: May I give you something for your soup? I have some corn in the sack on my donkey.

All: That would be good!

Part III

Narrator: The wind rattled the boards on the barn. The rain fell harder. Under the shed the friends sat and talked. They shucked the corn and scraped it into the simmering soup. They looked up as one more traveler led a horse into the barn. Streams of water fell from his hat.

Miller: Hello, Doctor! You do not live near here. What are you doing so far from home?

Doctor: I was visiting a sick man and could not ride home in the storm.

Will: Come and sit with us.

Narrator: The doctor wiped his eyes and looked into the pot. He sniffed the simmering soup.

Doctor: What a good smell! What is it?

All: "Making do" soup!

Ben: You start with water, . . .

Will: and chop in a potato, . . .

Farmer: and add some beans, . . .

Miller: and some corn!

Narrator: The doctor scratched his head.

Doctor: Hmmm. The man I visited gave me something that is just what you need for your soup.

80

Narrator: The doctor went to his horse. He came back with a big chunk of meat. He dropped it into the pot.

All: Meat!

Narrator: They let the soup simmer until it was finished. Then everyone ate as much as he wanted. Later, when everyone was asleep, Will sat up and stretched.

Will: Ben?

Ben: Yes, Will?

Will: Making do is not so bad after all.
And, Ben, . . .

Ben: Yes, Will?

Will: I will try not to grumble so much
from now on.

Ben: GOOD!

CREATURES GREAT & SMALL

A Ribbon for Cocoa
The Best Cow

As the sun rose over the trees, Pete jumped out of bed. He dressed quickly. He had no time to be lazy.

"Just one more day until the big contest," he was thinking. "I hope Cocoa will win a prize. I must scrub her coat well today. Then she will look like brown velvet. She will be the best-looking cow at the fair."

Smiling and singing, Pete ran to the kitchen. "Good morning, Mom and Dad," he said. "Can we go now? Cocoa needs something to eat."

"And so do you! Eat quickly and then we will go," said Dad, grinning.

The drive to the fair was short, but it did not seem short to Pete. At last they reached the fair.

Pete was so eager to see Cocoa that he ran all the way to her stall. Her big brown eyes seemed to say, "Good morning. Did you forget me? What do I get to eat?"

"You are the best cow," Pete said. He gave Cocoa a fork load of hay and patted her sleek brown coat. Then he whispered in her ear, "I want you to win a ribbon!"

A Clean Cow

With a bucket of brushes and soap in one hand, Pete led Cocoa away to give her a bath. Getting her wet was fun. "This soap will make your coat shine," Pete said as he rubbed.

The next thing to clean was Cocoa's swishing tail. Pete dropped the brush into the bucket of soapy water. As he bent to pick up the brush, Cocoa began playing a game. Pete heard her tail go swish, swish! Soapsuds and water went everywhere, splashing Pete all over.

"Stop that!" Pete ordered. Soap suds dripped past his eyes and dribbled off his chin. Cocoa just looked at him with her big brown eyes.

With the tail finished at last, Pete said, "I get my ears cleaned. You must get your ears cleaned too." Taking the rag, he scrubbed her ears.

Back to the barn they went. Cocoa was clean and shiny, but Pete was not. Cocoa was wet and so was Pete.

"It is time to rest," Pete said. While he waited for Cocoa to dry, he sat on the ground. A family stopped to see Pete's cow.

"Does a brown cow give chocolate milk?" a little lad asked.

"No," said Pete smiling. "Some cows are brown. Some are black and white. Some are red, but every cow gives white milk."

Pete spent the rest of the day showing Cocoa to the other people that came by. He liked to hear them say what a fine cow she was.

But Pete was afraid Cocoa would not win a ribbon. "What if she does not get any prize at all?" he began to think. "What will Dad say?"

Then Pete remembered Dad's favorite verse. "Whether therefore ye eat, or drink, or whatsoever ye do, do all to the glory of God."

Pete patted Cocoa on her back. "Dad would want us to do our best for the Lord," he said. "Get a good rest. I will see you in the morning!"

The Big Day

The next morning Pete sat up sleepily. Then he opened his eyes wide! "This is the big day!" he said to himself.

Pete could hardly wait to get to the fair, but he still remembered to bow his head and pray. "Lord, please help me to remember to trust You. Help Cocoa to win a prize if it's Your will." While he was dressing, Pete was thinking about Cocoa and the fair and the ribbons.

When Pete's family got to the fairgrounds, Pete ran to the barn. He greeted Cocoa with a happy "Good morning." Pete patted the cow's wide brown back, and then brushed her sides.

Dad walked with Pete and Cocoa to the ring. "I will be praying for you. Do a good job," he said.

Pete led Cocoa into the ring. He heard the crowd all around him. There were so many people! Then Pete saw a man standing in the middle of the ring. He saw some ribbons in the man's hand. Pete forgot all about the people. He forgot about everything but those ribbons. He began to dream about having one of the ribbons in his own hand.

Suddenly Pete remembered the verse that he had said to himself the day before. "Whether therefore ye eat, or drink, or whatsoever ye do, do all to the glory of God."

"Lord," Pete prayed, "help me to remember that it does not matter if Cocoa wins a ribbon or not. Help me to do my best for You."

Pete did not feel scared anymore. He waited.

Was the man with the ribbons saying his name? Pete looked at Dad. Dad was nodding and clapping. The man had just given Cocoa a red ribbon!

"We have a ribbon, Cocoa!" Pete hugged his prize-winning cow. "We did our best today!"

The Secret

We have a secret, just we three,
The robin, and I, and the sweet cherry tree;
The bird told the tree, and the tree told me,
And nobody knows it but just us three.

Clearly the robin knows it best.
She built the—I'll not tell the rest;
And laid the four small—something in it.
Oh, I fear I will tell it every minute.

But if the tree and the robin don't peep,
I'll try my best the secret to keep;
But when the little birds fly about,
Then the whole secret will be out.

—Author Unknown

Kangaroos and Koalas
Jumpers

What is your home like? Is it big or small? Is it made of bricks or logs? How many people live in it? Somehow, there is just no spot quite like home.

Some baby animals have homes that move. Their homes give them everything they need for eating, sleeping, and keeping dry. If you will read with me about some animals of Australia, I'll tell you about some of their homes.

A baby kangaroo's home is his mother's
pouch. He is very small when he is born.
Your littlest finger could be bigger than he
is! After sixteen weeks he will open his eyes
and peek out of his home. After twenty-five
weeks he will leave his mother's pouch. His
home will have become too small.

The kangaroo may grow to be seven feet
tall, not quite as tall as a wall in your
house. His tail will be more than three feet
long, about as tall as you are. His tail will
be very strong. It would not be good to be
in the way when he twitches that big tail!

The kangaroo's back legs are big and strong. With those strong legs he can hop very fast. He could even leap a wall that is nine feet tall or a puddle that is twenty-five feet wide. The kangaroo needs this speed and ability to help him get away from an enemy. But if he is cornered, he will use his strong back legs to protect himself. I've heard that one kick can kill an animal or even a man!

Kangaroos also use their legs for playing. What games do you like to play? Do you like to play tag? Kangaroos like to play tag too! But boxing is the game they like best. I do not think I would box with them. Would you?

Climbers

Here is one other baby that has a home that moves around. What does he look like to you? He may look like a stuffed animal, but he is not. This cuddly-looking animal is a koala.

Like the kangaroo, a koala is less than one inch long when he is born. He too will stay in his mother's pouch for twenty-five weeks. Then his mother will give him a ride on her back. Little by little he will become a strong climber. His sharp claws will help him hang on to the branches.

He will need those sharp claws for the rest of his life. Koalas spend all their time in eucalyptus trees. They never eat anything but eucalyptus leaves. And they always eat those by biting off a leaf at the stem. They eat the leaf from the bottom to the top. Do you think it would be good to eat the same thing every day?

In Australia, *koala* means "no drink."
Koalas do not drink much water. They get
all the water they need from the leaves of
trees. That is why koalas hardly ever come
down from the trees.

Koalas even sleep in the trees. They can
close their eyes and sleep on a branch. And
they will not fall off while they are sleeping!

It is fun to read about animals of other
lands! What do you remember about the
koalas and kangaroos? Ask your friends
about them to see what they remember.

Little Lost Lamb

(taken from Luke 15:4-7)

All but One

"Come, my flock," the shepherd called. "It is time to go home. It will be night before we get to the fold."

The shepherd led the way home. The sheep trusted him and followed closely. The little lambs ran by their mothers' sides. Puffs of dust filled the air as the many tiny feet trotted along the path.

All the sheep followed the shepherd—all but one.

106

One little lamb stopped to nibble on a clump of grass. Then he saw some greener clumps of grass a little farther away. The little lamb left the path to eat some of the good green grass. He nibbled another clump and then another. He heard the other sheep going home, but he kept straying farther and farther away.

The rest of the flock trotted over the hill back to where they lived. The little lamb was all alone.

One Is Missing

"Sixty-one, sixty-two, sixty-three," the shepherd said as he counted the sheep. The sheep trotted past him into the fold.

The shepherd and his sheep were safe at home. Here the strong stone wall would keep the flock until morning. Here the robbers could not steal the flock. Here the animals could not kill the sheep.

The shepherd counted the last of the flock. "Ninety-seven, ninety-eight, ninety-nine." There were no more sheep to go in.

"One lamb is missing," said the shepherd. "Where could he be? Maybe his leg is cut. Or robbers may have tried to steal him. An animal may even have snatched him away."

"I must go look for the lost lamb!" the shepherd exclaimed.

As the shepherd left to look for the lamb, the sky became dark. The ninety-nine sheep were safe in the fold. One stray lamb was not.

Storm clouds were filling the sky now. Far away the thunder rumbled. The wind began to blow very hard. Still the shepherd looked. He could not see the little lost lamb anywhere.

The shepherd called out to the lamb and then listened for the lamb's cry.

By now raindrops were pounding on the ground. Drawing his cloak closer, the wet shepherd struggled along.

Somewhere out in the storm was a little lost lamb.

"Baa, baa." The shepherd heard the faint cries from far away.

"That must be my stray lamb," said the shepherd.

Found

The shepherd left the path. He climbed over the rocks. Still he could not find the lamb.

"Baa, baa," came the cries again, closer this time.

The shepherd looked down the side of a
steep cliff. There caught on a rock below
was the little lamb. The frightened lamb lay
by the side of the cliff. Just one more step
and the lamb would fall.

The shepherd lowered his staff and lifted
the lamb.

The little lamb's fluffy white coat was now tattered and torn. Thorns had ripped his soft fluff.

"I'm glad the wild beasts did not find you before I did," said the shepherd.

With the lamb in his arms, the shepherd started home. The storm had passed.

When they were safe at home, the kind shepherd began to clean the bleeding cuts. After each cut was cleaned, the shepherd rubbed the lamb's little head.

The little lamb snuggled down close to the sheep in the fold. With sleepy eyes the lamb looked to the shepherd as if to say, "It is good to be inside the fold."

The happy shepherd ran to tell his friends. "Come and give thanks with me," he shouted. "I've found my lost lamb."

The shepherd and his friends met to give thanks and praise. The little lamb was home at last.

Kate Kangaroo

Work to Do

The sun shone brightly into the Kangaroos' grass hut.

"Kate," Kit called. "Time to get up."

Kate groaned. "Go away, Kit."

Kit hopped to the kitchen. Mom was baking muffins. Dad was reading the paper.

When the muffins were baked, Dad called Kate. She hopped slowly to her seat, yawning and stretching.

After they had all eaten, Dad said, "We have work to do today. Who will help me?"

"I will," said Kit.

"I will," said Kate.

Mom made box lunches for the three workers. Off they hopped to a grassy plot of land. The grass there was taller than Dad.

"Our roof is getting holes in it," Dad said. "We must cut this grass to put on the roof."

They began snipping. Kate snipped fast. She tied up a big bundle of grass.

"I'm tired," she said to herself. "I'll take a swim in the pool." Kate did not finish her job. She hopped to the pool, leaving her bundle behind.

At noon Dad stopped for lunch. "Where is Kate?" he asked.

"Here I am," Kate called, shaking off water at every hop. "I'll get my bundle of grass."

But when she looked, she could not find it anywhere. A grasshopper sat munching on a blade of grass where Kate had left the bundle. "Have you seen my bundle of grass?" Kate asked.

The grasshopper nodded. "Was that yours? It was not for lunch? My friends and I just finished eating it."

"Oh, no!" Kate hopped sadly back to Kit and Dad. She explained what had happened. "I'll help more this afternoon," she said.

Kate Stops Again

The kangaroos ate their lunches. Then Dad picked up his grass bundles. "Now we have to fix the roof. Who will help me?"

"We will," said Kit and Kate. Kit picked up his bundle.

Kate hopped happily down the path beside Dad and Kit. She would finish the job this time.

Dad climbed up the ladder to take off the torn roof. "I need some tar for the roof," he said. "Tar will keep out the rain."

"We will get it," Kate and Kit said. They each got a bucket and hopped to the tar pit. Quickly they filled the buckets with tar and began to drag them home.

But soon Kate hopped slower and slower.
The tar was sticky and smelly. It was hard
to carry the bucket down the road.

"Come on, Kate!" said Kit.

"You take your bucket to Dad. I will
rest for a while," said Kate.

"Do not take too long," called Kit as he
hopped away.

Kate stopped by a shady tree. "It is cool here," she said. She put her bucket down and stretched out on the grass. Soon she was sound asleep.

When Kit got back to the house, Dad put the tar on the roof. Just as he was about to tar Kate's room, the last of the tar dripped out of the bucket.

"I need more tar," he said. "Kate did not bring her bucket of tar back. She needs to understand that she must finish the jobs she begins."

Just then a raindrop hit his nose. Another fell in the empty bucket.

"We will not be able to tar Kate's room," said Dad. He climbed down the ladder. He and Kit rushed inside as the rain fell harder and harder.

A Lesson for Kate

The rain woke up Kate. She hopped home, leaving the tar bucket behind.

Kate went into the kitchen. Today was Mother's cleaning day. Kate was supposed to help fix supper. But the dishes from that morning lay piled in the sink. Kate had left them there.

Kate had not shelled the peas after Mother had picked them. The water pitcher sat on the counter waiting to be filled. Kate hopped into the living room. Dad, Mom, and Kit were talking about the work they had finished that day. Kate hung her head. She hopped quietly to her room.

Kate sat down in her chair to think. Plop! A drop of water fell on her foot. She looked down and saw a puddle at her feet. Raindrops fell on her bed and on her books. The tar on the roof kept the rain out of the rest of the house, but Kate's room had no tar over it.

Kate hopped into the living room. "Rain is coming in the house," she said. "The rest of the roof has tar on it, but my roof does not."

"I ran out of tar when you did not bring me your bucket," Dad said. "Stay in the living room and you will not get wet."

Kate sat in her chair. Her nose quivered sadly. The rain came down harder and harder.

Dad and Mom went to sleep. Even Kit fell asleep. But something was bothering Kate. She could not get any rest.

She remembered cutting the grass. She had not finished that job. She remembered getting the tar. She had not finished that job. "I never finish what I begin," she said sadly.

Finish What You Start

Kate hopped outside. The rain had stopped. Kate ran to get the tar bucket she had left by the tree. She climbed up the ladder. Quickly she dripped the tar on the roof of her room. She climbed back down and cleaned up the rain puddles in her room.

Everyone was still asleep.

Kate hopped to the kitchen. She cleaned out the sink and did the dishes. She shelled the peas and made a salad.

Kate set the table. She took the pitcher to the brook to get some fresh water.

Dad woke up. He heard Kate hop out of the kitchen. Kit and Mom heard her too. They jumped into the kitchen and looked around.

"Did Kate do this?" they asked each other.

Kate hopped in and set the pitcher of water on the table. "Hello," she said.

Mom smiled at Kate. "What did you do, Kate?"

Kate wiggled her tail so hard that it shook the table. "I've finished all the jobs I could think to do," she said.

Mom gave Kate a big hug. "I am proud of you, Kate!" she said.

"So am I," said Dad, smiling. "You have learned to finish the job!"

The Squirrel

Whisky, frisky,
Hippity hop,
Up he goes
To the tree top!

Whirly, twirly,
Round and round,
Down he scampers
To the ground.

Furly, curly,
What a tail!
Tall as a feather,
Broad as a sail!

Where's his supper?
In the shell,
Snappity, crackity,
Out it fell!

Author unknown

129

Cheerful Chickadees

The Chickadee Feeder

"Let's go for a walk in the woods," said Dad. "Get your coats and boots." Mother gave them their mittens and waved good-bye.

A Saturday walk in the woods with Dad was always fun. He showed them many things—foxes' dens, birds' nests, and rabbits' holes. They even saw raccoon tracks beside a frozen puddle of water.

"Look at that pine tree," Dad said. "Maybe you will see some good friends of mine." They stopped talking and stood still.

Before long, one little bird began to twitter, "Chick-a-dee-dee-dee." Soon many birds twittered around the tree. They pecked at the seeds in the pine cones.

"They all have tiny black hoods," Becky said.

"Yes, that is part of their name. They are called black-capped chickadees," Dad explained.

"Look!" Mark whispered, "One of them is hanging upside down."

"Will it fall?" Becky asked.

"No, it is hunting for insects in the bark," Dad said.

After a while they walked on. Becky and Mark began looking for chickadees. They counted sixteen of them, but they heard many more calling "chick-a-dee-dee-dee" from the treetops overhead.

At last they turned to go home.

They walked by the pine tree where the chickadees were feeding.

"Look how fat they have become!" Mark said.

Dad chuckled. "They have put on winter coats! They ruffle and puff out their feathers till they are snug as can be. The feathers trap hot air next to their skin and keep winter air out."

"Could we feed them?" Becky asked.

"I could make a bird feeder from a box," Mark said.

"Yes, that would be fine," Dad agreed.

At home Mark went right to work. He cut out two holes in the sides of a milk carton. Then he painted the outside dark green. Dad put a wire hook in the feeder. Mark hung it in a tree. Becky put in the seeds.

From the kitchen window Becky and Mark could peek at the feeder.

Chickadee Tamers

Many chickadees came to Becky and Mark's bird feeder. The birds twittered while Becky and Mark ate their oatmeal in the morning. The birds chirped while the children ate their sandwiches at lunch. But the chickadees ate the seeds between meals too. Becky had to put out seeds every day.

Sometimes Becky and Mark would sit in the yard when the chickadees came to the feeder. One day a chickadee sat on a branch of a cedar tree and looked at them. Mark whistled at it, and it seemed to whistle back.

Dad came outside and sat down beside Becky and Mark. The chickadees fluttered back and forth in the yard.

"Those chickadees have become tame," Dad said. "Do they land on your hand and take seeds yet?"

"They would eat out of our hands?" Mark asked.

"They might," Dad said.

Becky and Mark grabbed some seeds and ran to the feeder.

They waited and waited.

Then they heard a "Chick-a-dee-dee-dee."

A chickadee fluttered in a circle around Mark. It landed on his hand, took a seed, then fluttered away. Soon another one came and took one of Becky's seeds. It went to a tree and sang, "Chick-a-dee-dee-dee."

Mother peeked out the window and smiled. "Come inside," she called. "You must be freezing!"

Mother made hot apple cider. They all sat by the window to see the birds.

"It is snowing," Mother said.

"What will happen to the chickadees?" Becky asked.

"God takes care of all the animals, Becky," Dad said.

Mark smiled. "Dad, you said the chickadees ruffle their feathers and trap hot air inside them. Is that how God takes care of them?"

"Yes," Dad said, "God has given chickadees a way to protect themselves."

The snow fell all afternoon, but the chickadees twittered and played happily.

The snow kept falling all night.

Happy as a Chickadee

The next morning Becky and Mark woke up to a bright, white day. The sun had come out. The snowstorm had stopped.

Becky and Mark dressed and ate. Then they went outside to clean up the snow. The sun shone on the snow and made it sparkle like gems.

"If I were a giant, I would sneeze. Then all the snow would blow away!" Mark said.

Becky giggled. "But you are not a giant, Mark. You will have to clean up the snow anyway."

Mark brushed off the car. Becky cleaned the walk. "I'll clean the bird feeder," Mark said. He dusted off the snow. "Where are the chickadees today?" he asked. "I hope they did not freeze."

Just then they heard a "Chick-a-dee-dee-dee." In the cedar tree sat a little black-capped gentleman waiting for some seeds.

Becky ran inside to get some seeds. When she came back, she held them out to the chickadee.

It landed gently on her fingers and picked out a big seed. Then it fluttered back to the cedar tree.

"Chick-a-dee-dee-dee," it sang.

"Those chickadees are happy all the time," Becky said. "They never seem to grumble."

Mark put some seeds in the feeder. "When I see them singing in the snow, I feel like singing too," he said.

"Me too," said Becky. "I think I'll try to be as cheerful as a chickadee."

Make Your Own Bird Feeder

1. Clean a milk carton.

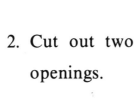

2. Cut out two openings.

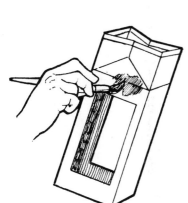

3. Paint the outside of the carton.

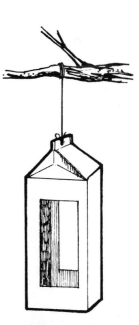

4. Ask Mother or Dad to put a wire hook in the top.

5. Put birdseed inside the feeder and hang it outside beside a window.

A Trip to Kruger Park

(a true story)

Off to Kruger Park

The Africans waved as the Bains got into their car.

"Good-bye," the Bains called to their African friends. The little blue car bumped down the road.

The Bains' missionary work in Africa was over. Leaving their friends was not easy. They had witnessed to many Africans. Some of them had trusted Christ to save them. Now God had another missionary job for the Bain family. They had to go back to America to prepare for this job.

But before they left Africa, they planned to visit Kruger Park to see the wild animals. Debby and David could hardly sit still.

"I'm glad we can go camping," Debby said.

"Me too," David agreed. "I hope we see elephants and baboons in the park!"

"We must keep our windows closed," Dad said as they got near Kruger Park. "The animals in the park are not in cages. They run wild. We do not want them coming into the car."

The edge of the park had tall poles around it with barbed wire strung on them. The little car drove in the gate.

"We must look out for elephants," Dad said. "Sometimes they tip over cars with their trunks. If they sit on our little car, it will be crushed.

Debby looked out the back window. No elephants were coming behind them. "I've heard that elephants cannot see very well. Will they see our little car?" Debby asked.

"They will smell us with their trunks," Dad explained. "They flap their large ears when they smell something. Then they come close to see it."

Dad drove the little car past tall grass. No other cars were around. The Bains looked for wild animals.

Elephants

"Is that an elephant?" Mother asked. A gray shape lumbered out of the trees.

Dad stopped driving. "I think it is," he said. "I hope it does not come any closer."

But the elephant trudged down the road closer and closer.

"It is not flapping its ears," Debby whispered to Mother.

145

Soon the elephant was very close. Then more elephants walked out of the trees from the left side of the road.

David began counting them. "Twenty-three!" he whispered.

"We had better leave!" Mother said.

"They do not smell us yet," Dad said. "We cannot leave too quickly. They might chase us. We do not want to be in the middle of an elephant stampede!"

Mother and the children began to pray.

Slowly, Dad backed the little car away.

One elephant flapped its ears. It stepped on the road.

Dad drove faster. The elephant flapped its ears faster. Its trunk flipped up and down sniffing for the car.

The elephant could not find them. At last it lumbered off into the trees. The other elephants followed.

"Thank you, Lord, for protecting us," Dad prayed.

The little car passed the spot where the elephants had stood. It bumped along down the dusty road.

"We need to get to camp before the sun sets," Mother said.

It was not long until the Bains saw the tent tops of the campground. The edge of the campground had barbed wire just like the edge of the park. This wire kept the animals out of the campground.

The family ate dinner outside. They gave tracts to the other campers. Then they went to bed on straw mats in the tent.

Sounds in the Night

The Bains had just fallen asleep when they heard loud sounds outside.

Crash! The tin trash can banged loudly as it fell over.

"Oh, no! Is it elephants?" Mrs. Bain asked. She peeked outside, but it was too dark to see anything.

The sound of something running between the tents sent shivers down Debby's back.

The Bains heard men yelling. At last the loud sounds stopped.

Mr. Bain went outside. The men were picking up the dented trash cans.

"What happened?" Mr. Bain asked.

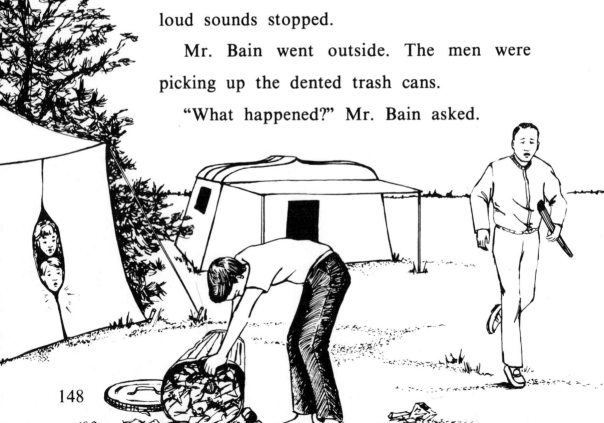

148

"Baboons climbed over the barbed wire and knocked down the trash cans," the men said.

"Baboons made those loud sounds?" Mr. Bain asked. "It was not elephants?"

"No, elephants cannot get into the campground," they replied.

Dad let Mother know what had happened. "Just some baboons," he said. "No elephants."

Mother sighed as she closed the tent flap. "Back to bed," she said to Debby and David.

The next day the little blue car bumped along again.

"Do you see the mud huts there?" Dad asked as they drove into the next campground. "We will sleep in a hut tonight. The Africans make the walls of thick mud. It dries hard and then even the rain cannot make it fall apart." Everyone slept soundly that night. They felt safe and snug in the sturdy huts.

Catching a Baboon

In the morning, the men in the campground showed the Bains how to make Putu porridge. The Bains gathered around the huge black pots as the porridge bubbled.

"Look," Debby said, turning to the camp tables. "A baboon is stealing a pumpkin from that table!"

No one had seen the sneaky baboon climb over the barbed wire. The baboon picked up the pumpkin in its mouth. Mr. Bain and the men began running to the fence. The baboon climbed back over the wire. The men ran faster. With a plunk the pumpkin fell. Big orange bits of pumpkin stuck in the baboon's teeth. Away to the trees ran the baboon, munching its stolen bits.

"We will catch one of those baboons," the men said.

One man chopped a small hole in the top of a gourd. He put peanuts inside and tied a rope around the thin neck of the gourd. The other end of the rope he tied to a tree. Then he hid in the grass. It was not long before another baboon climbed over the barbed wire.

The baboon hopped up to the gourd. He stuck a hairy paw inside to steal the peanuts.

A puzzled look came over the baboon's face. He tugged and screeched and screeched and tugged.

Debby giggled. "The baboon's fist has too many peanuts in it. If he were not so greedy, he could get his paw out."

The baboon would not let go of the peanuts. It hopped around, struggling to get free. The gourd hung from its arm. The African man slipped up and grabbed the baboon. Even then the baboon refused to let go of the peanuts.

Mr. Bain smiled at the sight of the silly baboon. "That baboon reminds me of something," he said. "Those peanuts are like sin in our lives. Sometimes we do not want to give up sin. We want to keep it, just like the baboon wanted to keep those peanuts."

The Bains waved good-bye to the men at the campground.

"I'll miss Africa when we go back to America," Debby said. "I'm glad we are missionaries. I like telling Africans about Christ. And I'll never forget that baboon trying to get those peanuts!"

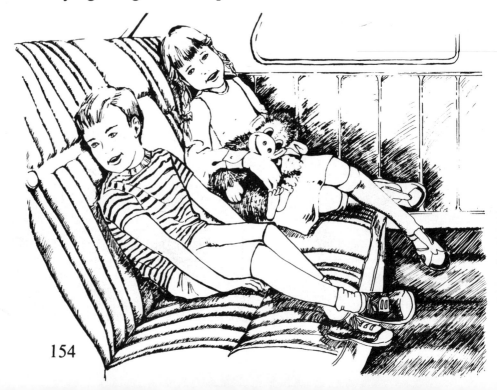

Who Needs a Bath?

(based on a true story)

"Uncle" Mac

Each day on the ranch began with noise. Meowing kittens, bleating lambs, and clucking chickens joined their voices in the same song. Each one waited and hoped to be fed first.

Mother went into the barn. Mac, the family dog, came running from the darkness. Jumping up and down beside Mother, he begged for something to eat. After that he would work. Mother put food and water out for him. Mac gulped it down.

Mac was an eager helper. He felt it was his job to take care of all the little animals.

As each little lamb finished his milk, he stood waiting for Mac. Mac trotted over to the lambs and started licking their fuzzy faces.

Not one squawk was heard as Mac began licking the baby chickens. Each fluffy feather was licked into place. Mac did not even think about eating the chicks. He just wanted to help.

Cleaning faces kept Mac running. Meowing kittens were now calling to Mac. They were waiting for their turn. Fluffy faces peeked over the top of the orange crate. Their black fur was speckled white with milk.

Mother Cat jumped from the box and ran off. It was time for her to hunt. She had to find food to eat. Mac would stay with the kittens. He would take care of them. He would keep them from harm.

Where Is Mac?

With short, quick licks Mac cleaned the kittens' sticky faces. Getting their fur and faces cleaned by "Uncle" Mac was fun. Each gentle lick sent another tiny kitten tumbling.

Mac pranced about with his tail up in a happy little curve. Smoky, the big horse, came close. A look of envy gleamed in his eyes.

Smoky stared at Mac. Mac stared at Smoky. Each one was waiting.

Then the horse leaped and nipped at Mac. The flashing teeth grabbed Mac's tail just for a moment, then let go.

Mac did not seem to enjoy the game. He let out a loud yelp. His tail was not hurt, but he wanted others to think so.

Mac liked to stay near the little animals. But one day he was missing. He was not in the barn. He was not by the house. He was not anywhere to be seen.

Sue cried. "What if Mac got killed?"

"I do not think he did," replied Mother. "Mac is a good fighter."

The baby chickens seemed sad that Mac was not cleaning their feathers. The little lambs bleated and bleated. Mac was not there to lick the kittens' faces.

Sue began to cry. Mother put her arm around Sue. "We will look until we find Mac!" she said.

A Smelly Animal

The family began to look right away.

"Here, Mac!" they called. Mac still did not come running.

Sue decided to look in the big red barn for Mac. But he was not there. Dad rode by the garden in the truck. Mac was not there.

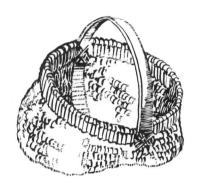

Mother took the basket for the eggs. She would look in the chicken coop. It was the last place she could think of to look. Suddenly she stopped by the corncrib. "What is that awful smell?" She sniffed the air.

"I did not find Mac, but I did find a skunk," she said to herself. "That skunk cannot stay here. He will eat all my chicken eggs."

Mother grabbed a long stick. She began to poke around in the hole under the corncrib. Two shiny eyes peeked out.

Then she heard something whine. Slowly, that something began to wiggle out from under the corncrib.

With one last big tug, out came the animal. It tumbled over and over in the grass. It scratched at its nose as if to rub away the smell. Then it jumped up and ran to Mother.

"Oh!" squealed Mother. She tried to dodge the barking, smelly dog. "I know what happened to you, Mac!" she said as she held her nose.

Begging brown eyes looked up.

Mother grinned. "That will teach you not to lick every face you see. I hope you chased that skunk away. Now it is your turn to get a bath."

Mother called to Dad and Sue. "We have a job to do!"

The Crow and the Pitcher

A wren sat in a tree. He saw a crow hopping along the dusty road below him.

"I'm tired and thirsty," the crow called to the wren. "There isn't a drop of water anywhere."

"Do you see that orange pitcher over there in the grass?" asked the wren. "Maybe it still has some water in it."

"Aren't you thirsty too?" asked the crow.

"No," replied the wren. "I found some water this morning."

The crow flapped his wings and ruffled his dusty feathers. He hopped slowly to the pitcher. Deep inside lay some water. The crow stuck his beak in to drink some, but he could not reach the water.

"If I tip it, the water will spill on the ground and be lost," he said. He hopped away to think.

"I know!" he cried.

The crow picked up a round pebble in his beak. Plunk! He dropped it into the pitcher. The water didn't seem to move. He picked up another and another and put them in. Plunk, plunk! The water seemed a little higher. Plunk, plunk, plunk! The crow worked very hard. Bit by bit the water crept to the top. At last the crow could stick his beak in and take a long drink.

"You can always find a way when you must," called the wren from his tree.

Wolf Pack

(a true story)

Happy Birthday

Welcome to Lapland. It is winter here now. The woods and hills are still under the snow. The streams and lakes are filled with ice. The sky doesn't stay light for long. When it is dark, the wolves come out for food. I am glad I am safe at home by then!

Yesterday was my birthday. I haven't ever had a birthday as exciting as the one yesterday. I think I was the happiest girl in Lapland.

166

When morning rays of sunshine lit up the sky, Mother and Father tiptoed into the kitchen. I was sleeping on a wooden bed in the corner.

My sleepy eyes opened when I heard them singing. Mother and Father were standing at my bedside. Their eyes sparkled as they sang a song to wake me.

In her hands Mother held my birthday tray. She put it on my bed. Cookies, coffee, and lighted candles were on the tray. Father was carrying the gifts.

Waiting to open the gifts was hard. When my treat was finished, I picked up the first present. It was soft. The paper crackled and crunched as I tore it off. Inside was a bright red stocking cap. Mother had knitted it for me. It was a perfect fit. The big tassel on top bounced as I walked.

Next I opened the big gift. Father had made a sled for me. The sled was painted red to match my cap. What fun it would be to go sledding down the hill!

"Thank you, Mother and Father. This is really a happy birthday," I said as I smiled.

Mother said my smile was so big she could not see my face. Somehow, I know my smile did not hide my eyes.

Sledding

Before Father left for his job, we sat down for Bible reading. Then we prayed as we did every morning. With his deep voice Father began reading a verse. "He shall call upon me, and I will answer him. I will be with him in trouble." For some reason, that verse stuck in my mind.

It wasn't long before I was dressed and out in the snow. The tassel on my red cap bounced as I dashed off with my sled. I played on the frozen lake beside the house. I had to be careful not to fall into the holes. Father had cut them last night to get water for the animals.

After lunch I decided to try riding my
sled down the hill. Up, up I went, dragging
the sled behind me. The top was not far
away now. The white valley and the lake
spread before me. Then I heard a howl.
Anyone in Lapland knows the howl of
hungry wolves. Chills ran up and down my
back as the dreaded cry came again.

A wolf doesn't often come out in the
daytime. This howl could mean just one
thing. These wolves were looking for dinner.

Wolves

As I turned I saw the wolves by the edge of the woods. I saw one and then another and another. There were at least six wolves. Their eyes flashed as they began to run toward me. The biggest wolf led the pack.

I flung myself on my sled. As I sped down the icy hillside, I remembered the Bible verse Father had read after breakfast. "He shall call upon me, and I will answer him. I will be with him in trouble."

"Dear Lord," I prayed, "please help me not to be afraid. Keep me safe. Amen."

The verse said God would take care of me. I just didn't know how He would do it. Ahead of me lay the shiny lake and the safety of home. Behind me I could hear the heavy breathing of the wolves.

174

I thought I could reach the lake beside the house. The sled would slide easily on the ice. But I didn't know what might happen next.

Crash! Splash, splash, splash! What a loud noise!

Mother came running. I had fallen off my sled. Ouch! What a bump on my head!

Mother knelt and put her arms around me. "God is so good to us!" she said. "The wolves fell into the holes Father cut for water last night."

"You are right, Mother," I agreed. "God was very good to me on my birthday. You gave me a red cap. Father gave me a fast sled. And God gave me the verse I needed even before I needed it. This will be a birthday I will never forget!"

Off to See the King

Cast:

Lemmy Lamb: Narrator

Billy Blow: wind

Red Comb: a rooster

Nicky Knife: knife

Big Splash: lake

Crumb Catchers: ants

Lion

King (Elephant)

Part I

Lemmy Lamb: A long, long time ago there lived a happy rooster in the kingdom of Kam. Day after day he scratched for bugs in the barnyard. Then one day his friend, the wind, came to visit.

176

Billy Blow: I have blown everywhere in the kingdom but I have never seen the king. I am going to visit him today.

Red Comb: Cock-a-doodle-doodle-doo, I would like to see him too.

Billy Blow: Then come with me!

Lemmy Lamb: Red Comb thought for a moment. Then he cocked his head.

Red Comb: Cock-a-doodle-doodle-doo, I will gladly go with you.

177

Lemmy Lamb: Off went the rooster and his friend. The rooster crowed and the wind whistled as they went. They had not traveled far before they came to a knife stuck in an oak tree.

Nicky Knife: Help! Help! A boy left me in this tree and now I cannot get loose.

178

Lemmy Lamb: Quickly the rooster jerked the knife free.

Nicky Knife: Where are you going?

Billy Blow: We are off to see the king.

Nicky Knife: I would like to see the king too. I will go with you.

Part II

Lemmy Lamb: The three friends went on down the road. They had not traveled much farther before they heard a loud moaning and groaning. They stopped beside a lake.

Nicky Knife: What is wrong?

Big Splash: Oh me, oh my! It rained all week, and now I have too much water in me.

Billy Blow: I will help you!

Lemmy Lamb: The wind began to blow and blow. Soon he had gathered up the extra water in the lake. It hung in a big cloud high in the sky. The three friends then went on down the road. They had not traveled far before they came upon some ants by the roadside.

Crumb Catchers: Help us! Help us! We do not have anything to eat.

Lemmy Lamb: Rooster Red Comb opened his bag and put the food down for the ants. In no time they had eaten all of it. The rooster, the wind with the water, the knife and the ants set off down the road. By and by they reached a thick forest.

Nicky Knife: Do we have to go through that forest?

Billy Blow: We have to do it to get to the king.

Lemmy Lamb: The friends stayed close together. They had not traveled far before a lion leaped from behind a tree. He grabbed the rooster as the others ran to hide.

Lion: Ah ha! I have caught my dinner!

Lemmy Lamb: He tied the rooster to a tree and went to look for a big pot.

Red Comb: Cock-a-doodle-doodle-doo, I would like some help from you!

Lemmy Lamb: The knife heard the rooster crow. He came quickly to help the rooster.

Nicky Knife: When I was stuck in a tree, you got me out. Now it's my turn to help you.

Lemmy Lamb: The knife cut the ropes. Just then the lion came running out of the trees. The little rooster ran as fast as he could. But the lion was too quick. Soon the little rooster was caught again.

Part III

Lion: I have caught you again! This time I believe I will roast you over the fire!

Red Comb: Cock-a-doodle-doodle-doo, I would like some help from you!

Lemmy Lamb: The wind heard the rooster's call. He huffed and he puffed until the cloud was over the fire.

Billy Blow: Cloud, send the water from Big Splash down and put out the fire!

Lemmy Lamb: With that, huge raindrops fell from the cloud. Faster and faster they came until the orange flames had died. Then the wind lifted the brave little rooster to the safety of a nearby tree.

Lion: You will not escape from me. I will get you down from there!

Lemmy Lamb: The lion clawed at the tree trunk. The little rooster began to shake. Then he remembered his friends, the ants.

Red Comb: Cock-a-doodle-doodle-doo, I would like some help from you!

Lemmy Lamb: The ants heard him call. Together they headed toward the lion.

Crumb Catchers: We will help you! We will bite that lion and make him run like a thief!

Lemmy Lamb: The ants bit the lion. He began to roar and jump, for the ant bites burned like fire. He shook off the ants and ran out of the woods.

Red Comb: Cock-a-doodle-doodle-doo, I have friends and so do you.

Lemmy Lamb: The friends set off down the road. Soon they were out of the dark forest and on their way to see the king.

Billy Blow: There is the town below us.

Lemmy Lamb: The friends walked down the hill and through the town. Everywhere they looked they saw animals. The animals stood on street corners. They even stood in the street.

Nicky Knife: Has everyone in the kingdom come to see the king today?

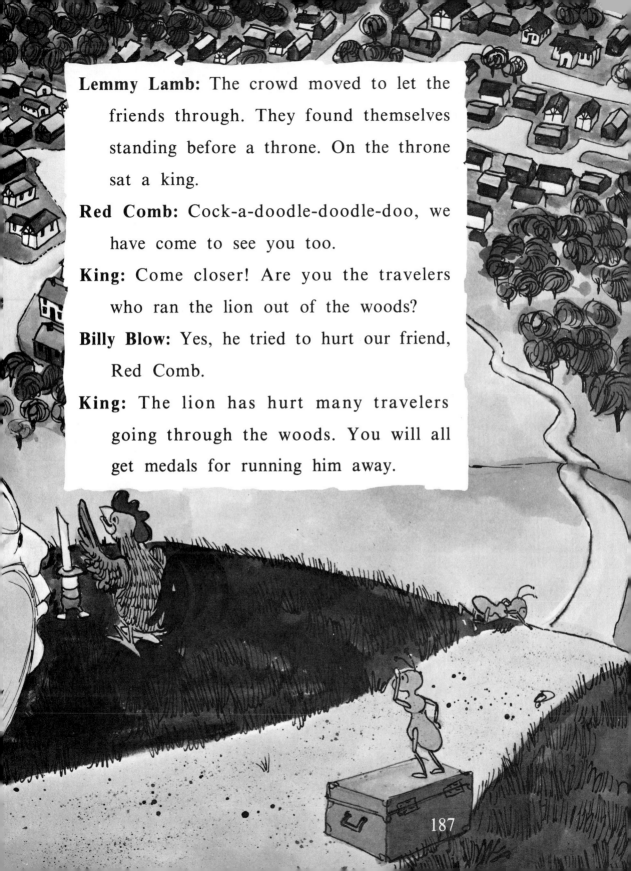

Lemmy Lamb: The crowd moved to let the friends through. They found themselves standing before a throne. On the throne sat a king.

Red Comb: Cock-a-doodle-doodle-doo, we have come to see you too.

King: Come closer! Are you the travelers who ran the lion out of the woods?

Billy Blow: Yes, he tried to hurt our friend, Red Comb.

King: The lion has hurt many travelers going through the woods. You will all get medals for running him away.

187

Lemmy Lamb: And the king gave each friend a big medal. The friends ate at the king's table and slept at the king's house. But at last it was time to go home. The friends waved good-bye.

King: Come back and visit me again.

Red Comb: Cock-a-doodle-doodle-doo, we will gladly visit you.

Lemmy Lamb: Then side by side, the friends began the trip home.

TREASURES

Candy and the Heathen

(based on historical research)

Five Cents

Jonathan Goforth was born on his father's farm in Canada in 1859. He had nine brothers and one sister. Those years in Canada were hard ones for everyone. Many people could not pay men to help work on the farms. It was a big help to Jonathan's family to have so many children. They all helped do the work on the farm.

When Jonathan was just a boy, a friend
came to visit.

"Would you like to see my chickens?"
Jonathan asked the visitor.

"That would be very nice," the lady
replied. So after lunch Jonathan took her
through the chicken house.

Soon the visitor was ready to leave. But just before the buggy rolled out of the yard, she gave him five pennies.

What a surprise! Jonathan had never had five cents of his own before.

"Mother!" he called. He ran up the steps, holding the five cents tightly. "The lady gave me five pennies! May I go to the candy store?"

"No, Jonathan," replied his mother. "You cannot go today."

Jonathan looked at his mother with pleading eyes. "Please," he begged.

"Jonathan, I know how you feel," his mother told him. "It was good of our visitor to give you five cents. But, look!" She gently turned Jonathan toward the road. The sky over the dark trees was pink. It was nearly time for the sun to go down.

"I see, Mother," he said sadly. "It will soon be dark." Jonathan was not old enough to walk to town in the dark.

"I'll go first thing in the morning!" he said. "I'll get up before daylight and do my chores!"

"Not in the morning, Jonathan. It's the Lord's Day," reminded his mother. "You will have to wait until next week. You can spend your five cents then." Jonathan's mother gave him a hug and went inside the house.

The Candy Store

Jonathan sat down on the steps and leaned on the post. He didn't see the sky turn from pink to red. He didn't hear the wind in the trees.

All he could see in his mind was the candy store. He felt the five cents in his pocket.

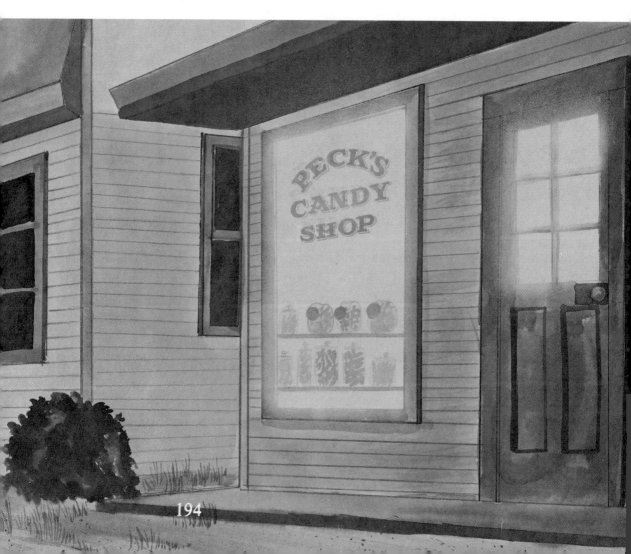

In his mind he walked down the street to the candy store. He could hear the bell jingle as he walked inside. He could feel the pine boards under his bare feet. He could see the jars and jars of candy. There were lemon drops, orange suckers, and peppermint sticks. There was almost everything a boy could wish for. For five cents he could get ten sticks of candy!

"Let me see," he thought to himself. "I want ten different sticks. I'll start with peppermint, and then—"

Just then Jonathan remembered something! He sat up straight. There would be an offering taken Sunday. It would be used to help lead the heathen to Christ!

Jonathan had forgotten all about the offering. He wished he had not remembered.

"I do not know any heathen," thought Jonathan. But he did know where the candy store was. It was two miles away.

Jonathan leaned on the post and went back to choosing his candy.

"I'll have peppermint," he said to himself, "and lemon, and . . ."

Jonathan smiled as he thought about all the different kinds of candy in the store.

The Battle

That night Jonathan put his five pennies on the table near his bed. Mother came to his room to tuck him in.

"Have you prayed yet, Jonathan?" Mother asked.

"No, Mother. I do not feel like praying tonight."

"Why not?" asked Mother.

"I do not know," replied Jonathan.

"Maybe there is something you need to get right with the Lord," said Mother.

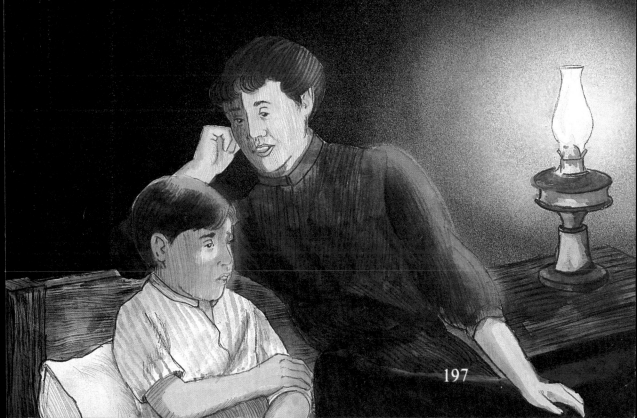

Jonathan hung his head. After Mother left, Jonathan tried three times to pray. But the most he could say was, "Dear Lord. . ."

Jonathan tossed and turned in his bed. He thought about the heathen. He thought about the candy. He pounded his pillow into a lump and tried to sleep. Still he lay with his eyes open.

The heathen and the candy—around and around the thoughts went in his head. Jonathan wanted that candy. But the heathen needed to hear about God.

"I'll give my five cents to the Lord," he decided. At last he was able to pray. Then he went to sleep, content with what he had decided to do.

The sunshine woke Jonathan the next morning. He jumped out of bed and ran to the window. It was a bright summer morning. He could see his little colt running through the grass. He could hear the rattle of milk pails as his brothers went about their chores in the barn.

"I slept late!" he thought as he dressed and ran to join them. He had to work quickly to finish his chores.

He was the last one to slide into his place at the table.

"You are a little late today," said his father.

"Yes, sir. I slept late," replied Jonathan.

"Did you sleep well last night?" Mother asked.

"Oh, yes, Mother," replied Jonathan happily.

Mother smiled at him.

The Offering Basket

When Jonathan was dressing for church, he saw the five pennies on the table. He picked them up to put them in his pocket. For a moment Jonathan held them in his hand. He could almost taste the candy he wanted.

"Jonathan!" called his father.

Jonathan stuffed the pennies into his pocket as he ran outside. His brothers grabbed his arms and lifted him into the wagon. Then the wagon left, heading toward the church.

Jonathan held on to keep from falling out. He did not hear the happy chatter of his family. Jonathan was thinking about the heathen and the candy again.

When they reached the church, Jonathan was still fighting his battle. He thought about the pennies all through the songs. He wanted that candy!

At last the time came to pass the offering basket. Jonathan's head hung lower and lower.

Jonathan could hear clink after clink as people dropped in their offerings. At last the basket reached his bench. Jonathan held his pennies tighter. He saw the basket pass down his family's row from brother to brother. It seemed to Jonathan that everyone had something to give. At last the basket reached him. He looked at the basket in his brother's hand. Slowly he opened his hand. He dropped in one penny, two pennies, three, four, five!

At each clink, Jonathan felt better. He forgot all about the candy he had wanted so much.

As he passed the offering basket along to the next person, he looked up. His mother looked at him and smiled. Jonathan grinned back from ear to ear.

How good it felt to give all he had to God!

The Flag Goes By

Hats off!
Along the street there comes
A blare of bugles, a ruffle of drums,
A flash of color beneath the sky:
Hats off!
The flag is passing by!

Blue and crimson and white it shines,
Over the steel-tipped, ordered lines.
Hats off!
The colors before us fly!

Henry Holcomb Bennett

Trail Treasures

Scout, the Treasure Hunter

Mother packed four peanut butter sandwiches, four red apples, and something to drink into Drew's knapsack. "Do not eat lunch until noon," she said.

Drew put a handful of dog biscuits in his treasure box. He tucked the box into his new knapsack with the lunch. Then he lifted the knapsack onto his back.

"We will not eat too soon," Drew said. "Bye, Mother. Come on, Jane."

"Come on, Eddie," Jane called to her little brother.

And Eddie called, "Come on, Sue."

"Bye," Mother said.

The children waved from the edge of the yard.

"What are you going to put in your treasure box?" Eddie asked.

"You will see!" Drew said. He whistled to his dog, Scout. Scout stretched and yawned, and then trotted after the children.

"Come on, Scout," Drew said, patting his dog's floppy ears. "What will you find for my treasure box today?"

Scout sniffed Drew's knapsack.

"Oh, you have found something already!" said Drew. He got out his treasure box and opened the lid a crack. "Here you go," he said as he threw Scout a dog biscuit.

"Ruff!" Scout barked.

Sue laughed. "I think that means 'Thank you,' " she said.

Scout chewed the biscuit and gulped it down quickly. Then he put his nose to the ground. He ran here and there sniffing and sniffing.

"What do you smell?" Drew asked. He looked at the ground. "Here is a trail to follow."

Scout ran down the trail and through the woods. "Ruff! Ruff!" he yelped.

Drew followed, then Jane, then Eddie, with Sue trailing along last of all. Her blue ribbons bounced as she tried to keep up.

At last Scout stopped under a pine tree. He jumped back and forth, barking and barking.

Drew slid under the low branches to get a better look. Before he knew it, he had slipped on the pine needles. "Ouch!" he cried, jerking a quill out of his hand. He looked at it closely. "Are you barking at a porcupine, Scout? You do not want to catch one of those!"

Drew slipped the porcupine quill into his treasure box.

Biscuits and Treasures

Before long Scout was running down another trail. Everyone hurried after him. Scout stopped to sniff at something on the ground.

"Ruff! Ruff!" came his deep bark. When the children caught up with him, Scout had something in his mouth. He dropped it at Drew's feet.

"What is it?" Jane asked.

Drew turned it over and over. "I think it is part of a deer antler."

Sue held it on top of her head as if she were a deer. The rest of the children laughed.

"What a treasure!" Drew said. "I hope it will fit into my treasure box."

He scooted all the dog biscuits to one side of the treasure box, but the piece of antler would not fit. Then he scooted them to the other side; still the piece of antler would not fit. Finally, he fed two of the biscuits to Scout. Then the antler fit into the box.

Drew reached into his knapsack and took out the lunches. "It is time for us to eat too," he said.

Scout had eaten three dog biscuits. That was enough for right now. He curled up at Drew's feet and fell asleep.

The children ate the sandwiches and fruit and drank their orange juice. Then they sat listening to the sounds of the forest.

The birds forgot that Drew, Jane, Eddie, Sue, and Scout were there. They began to chirp. A squirrel ran across the path and chattered at them. Drew tossed one of Scout's dog biscuits to it. It sat up on a nearby rock and nibbled on the biscuit.

Suddenly Scout's ears perked up.

"Ruff! Ruff!" he barked, his eyes suddenly wide open. A snake slithered from under some rocks.

"Oh, Scout!" Drew said. "It's only a blacksnake."

Scout barked again and jumped toward it. The snake slithered away.

Scout trotted across the path to the rocks. He sniffed at something caught between two of the rocks.

Drew went over to look. "Come and look," he called. "The snake shed its skin!" Everyone ran to look.

"How did he do that?" Sue asked.

"Snakes shed their old skin every now and then. The blacksnake may have shed his skin this morning. He probably used the rocks to help scratch it off," said Drew.

"May I put it in your treasure box?" Eddie asked.

"Yes," Drew said, and he opened his box wide.

214

More Treasures

"Scout is a good treasure finder," said Sue. "Would he find a treasure for me?"

Drew took out a dog biscuit. "Feed him this, Sue. Then he will find a treasure for you."

"Here, Scout," called Sue. She fed him the biscuit. "Ruff!" Scout barked. He ate it with a gulp. Barking, he ran off down the trail. When Sue caught up to him, he had something orange in his mouth.

"My old ball!" Sue exclaimed. She gave Scout a hug.

"I can carry your ball in my treasure box," Drew offered.

"May I try to get a treasure?" asked Eddie.

Drew handed him a biscuit. Eddie fed it to Scout, and Scout was off barking and yelping. Eddie ran right beside him.

Scout stopped at a tree. He barked at a hole by the tree roots. Eddie had seen a little brown mouse hop into it. He patted Scout's head. "No, Scout, I cannot keep that treasure." Then he saw a shape on the tree bark.

"Look!" he called. "An insect's skin!"

Drew picked it up. "Yes, it's a locust's skin. See where it split open down the middle. The locust is gone."

"Will you save it for me in your treasure box?" asked Eddie.

"Yes, I will put it on the antler so it will not get crushed."

"Is it my turn?" Jane asked. She threw the last biscuit to Scout. He caught the biscuit in the air and chewed it up.

"Ruff! Ruff!" he barked. Then he was off. Jane ran after him.

A bird flew down and twittered at Scout. He stopped to bark at it. Finally Jane caught up with him and stopped to catch her breath. She sat down on a log. There at her feet, right next to the log, lay part of a bird's eggshell.

Jane picked it up and called to the others. "Now I need a treasure box too! But will you keep it in yours for now, Drew?"

Drew placed the eggshell in his treasure box.

"I think we have enough treasures for now," said Drew. "It's time to go home."

Scout's Treasure

Far away the children heard the dinner bell ringing.

"Come on, Scout," said Jane.

Scout ran past the children. He barked every time he heard the dinner bell.

Before long the children passed Scout. He had found a new smell and was digging eagerly.

"Come on, Scout," the children called.

"Ruff! Ruff!" Scout barked. His paws dug faster.

"We cannot wait for you, Scout!" Drew said. "It's dinner time."

Drew, Jane, Eddie, and Sue raced into the yard. They ran up the steps and into the house. They found Mother in the kitchen.

"What did you find for your treasure box?" Mother asked.

The four children all began talking at the same time.

"Now, now," said Mother, smiling. "One at a time, please."

Drew took off his knapsack and got out the box. Everyone looked as Drew opened the treasure box. He lifted out the treasures one by one.

"This is Sue's treasure," he said.

"Yes, Scout found my orange ball," said Sue.

"This is Eddie's," said Drew.

Eddie took his locust skin. He held it up for Mother to see. "The locust outgrew its skin. See where it split this old one and crawled out?"

Mother looked closely.

"This is Jane's," said Drew.

Jane took her eggshell. "I wish I had the rest of it. Then I could try to glue it together."

"That would be a hard job," said Mother.

At last Drew showed his own treasures. Mother felt the sharp point of the porcupine quill and listened to Drew tell about the deer antler and the snakeskin.

"Do you have a box for my eggshell, Mother?" asked Jane.

"Yes," replied Mother. "After dinner I'll find enough boxes for all my treasure hunters. But right now we need to get ready to eat."

All the treasures went back into Drew's box.

"Where is Scout?" asked Mother. "He went with you, didn't he?"

"Yes," the children replied.

"He helped us find all of our treasures."

"Eddie, come and help me find him, please," said Drew. The two brothers hurried outside to look for Scout.

"Scout!" they called.

Scout came running out of the woods. He dropped something at Drew's feet. "Ruff! Ruff! Ruff!" he barked, as loudly as he could.

"A real bone!" Drew laughed. "Scout has found his own treasure. Now he does not need dog biscuits!"

Captain Stripe's Gold

The Trail

Zack Zebra trotted to the far end of the field. He tossed his head and looked back as the other zebras gathered around Captain Stripe.

"Stay out of the jungle!" he said to himself. "I get so tired of Captain Stripe's orders! Soon I will be the leader of the zebras. Then I can do as I wish."

He looked at the trail leading into the jungle. "I'm thirsty," he said to himself. He looked back at the muddy stream where the zebras were drinking.

"That water is too muddy to drink," he said, and trotted through the jungle. Branches hung over the trail, shutting out the bright sunlight.

Crack! Snap! Zack jumped as a huge head appeared between some branches. He looked at two big eyes and a long trunk.

"Where are you going?" asked Mumba, the elephant.

"I'm going to get something to drink," stammered Zack. He didn't want to say any more so he trotted quickly away.

Mumba stood still until the trees hid Zack from sight.

224

As Zack trotted farther into the jungle, the trail became overgrown with vines. Zack had to slow down and walk around them. At last he heard water dripping.

"Water!" he exclaimed, walking toward the sound. He stopped at the edge of the river and bent to drink.

"Psst!" hissed a voice. Zack looked up. There was no one to be seen.

"You aren't very friendly, are you?" hissed the voice. Zack jumped back as a large vine dropped down near him. Two yellow eyes looked into his.

"How about this, Croc?" the vine hissed. "Here is a striped horse that cannot talk!"

A log floated in the water near Zack's legs. It opened its eyes and looked at Zack sleepily.

"Cannot talk? What kind of beast is it?" it yawned.

Logs and vines that talk! Zack turned around quickly.

"Do not run away," hissed the voice. "We will not hurt you. I'm Mona, the python," the voice continued. "This is my friend, Croc. We do not get many visitors down here, do we, Croc?"

The crocodile sank a little lower in the water. "Not often enough anyway," he muttered with a hungry look in his eyes.

226

Gold!

Croc looked at the zebra. "What are you doing in this part of the jungle?"

"I needed a drink," replied Zack, tossing his head. "I'm very thirsty."

"By all means drink until you are done," hissed Mona. She coiled up around another branch.

Zack stretched his neck carefully to drink from the river. "This river is nice," he said. "We just have brooks to drink from back in the fields. The water is often muddy from so many hooves walking in it. Why do you two have this river all to yourselves?" he asked.

"Well," Mona lied quickly, "there are so many rivers here that everyone has his own watering place."

"Really?" asked Zack. "Why, this part of the jungle would be just the place for Captain Stripe. He's always looking for new watering places. Why doesn't he bring us here?"

The crocodile rolled his eyes at Mona. "Maybe he doesn't want you to know about the gold," he said.

"Gold?" asked Zack.

Mona swayed back and forth. "Oh, I thought everyone knew about the gold. Robbers hid it in a shady place many years ago. Now the vines have hidden it from sight. But I know where it is." Her eyes glowed.

"All we need is a strong fellow like you to get it for us," said Croc. "We will gladly share the gold with you."

Zack looked at the two friends. There was something about the pair that bothered him. Zack almost seemed to hear Captain Stripe talking. He shook his head and put the voice out of his mind.

"Where is the gold?" he asked. "I'll help you get it. I'll take real gold to the zebras. They will not think Captain Stripe's words are so good then! I will not have to wait until I am older to be the leader!"

"You must cross the bridge to the other side of the river," said Mona.

Zack looked at the old wooden bridge swaying across the river. "I do not think . . ." he began.

But Mona just laughed. "Are you really afraid? A leader cannot be afraid. It's a short trip. Soon you will be back with the gold."

The crocodile winked at Mona. "Bigger beasts than you have used the bridge."

Real Gold

Zack put one hoof on the bridge, then another one. The planks clattered under him as he moved. Creak! went the next board. He moved carefully on the bridge. But there were no boards for the next step. Zack looked down. He saw the hooded eyes of the crocodile looking up at him.

Zack stopped. Captain Stripe's words were clearer now. He tried hard to remember. The Captain had told the zebras why they should not go into the jungle.

232

"Come on! It's not far now." Croc blinked his yellow eyes.

The yellow eyes! That was it! Captain Stripe had said to never go near the yellow-eyed crocodile or his friend the python!

Zack backed off the sagging bridge. The empty bridge swayed back and forth. Suddenly it broke with a snap! Down it splashed into the water. The crocodile's mouth sprang shut on a plank.

"Ouch!" he cried, sinking into the water.

Zack turned around just as Mona dropped over him. He kicked and kicked, but she coiled around him tightly. There was no way to get loose from her grasp.

"Oh, Captain Stripe," he thought to himself, "your words were better than real gold! How I wish I had listened to you!"

"Stop!" thundered a voice. Zack looked up at the huge elephant he had seen by the trail.

"Go away," Mona hissed.

"Let him go," cried Mumba. "I could crush the likes of you under one of my feet."

He lifted one foot. Mona unwound slowly. She glared at the elephant and slithered away.

"There will be another time," she hissed and was gone.

Mumba turned to Zack. "Is this where you came to drink? I thought Captain Stripe kept you all in the fields. There you would be safe from Mona and Croc."

"He does," replied Zack meekly. "But I thought I was wiser than Captain Stripe. Now I know why he is the captain of the zebras and I'm not."

Mumba shook his head. "Captain Stripe thinks of your safety. He is a wise leader."

"I know now," Zack said. "I see why the other zebras listen to his words as if they were gold. They were better than real gold today."

"How much better is it to get wisdom than gold! and to get understanding rather to be chosen than silver!" **Proverbs 16:16**

236

Special Dogs

Dogs can be special friends and play-mates. They like to run and jump and fetch sticks that are thrown for them. But some dogs are much more than playmates. They have special jobs to do because God made them in special ways.

A blind person needs a dog that is gentle and smart. The golden retriever is one dog that is often used as a Seeing Eye dog for the blind. He is quick to sense danger for his master and to lead him around difficult spots. But a golden retriever is not always used to help the blind. He is also used for hunting.

God gave the retriever a thick undercoat of hair. It is almost waterproof! When a hunter shoots a bird as it flies over a pond, the retriever dives into the cold water. When he returns with the bird and lays it at the hunter's feet, he can shake himself almost dry.

Another good bird dog is the English setter. He is smart and hardworking on the field. He is a gentle dog so he makes a good pet. But it would not be good to keep him penned up. He is a restless dog and needs to run a lot. All this energy helps make him a tireless hunter!

See the pointer's tail? It sticks up high
so his master can find him in the tall grass.
Even when he is a puppy, the pointer likes
to hunt. When he is grown, he is a good
hunter. The pointer keeps his mind on his
job and tries to do his best. He works hard
and does not get tired easily. He works well
even with someone who is not his master.
He thinks his work is fun!

The small but smart Shih Tzu is not a good hunter, but he is a brave dog that will protect his master. He makes a fine show dog too. See how lively and alert he is. The Shih Tzus were kept as house pets by Chinese emperors. The name *Shih Tzu* is Chinese and means "lion." Do you think he looks like a tiny lion? Chinese men held contests to decide who raised the best Shih Tzu.

The emperor himself would choose the best one. The Emperor would have a picture painted of the dog. When it was done, he would hang it on the wall. The man who raised the dog would receive gifts from the emperor. Perhaps that's why the Shih Tzu looks so proud with its head held high!

The dogs in this picture may not have a keen sense of smell like the hunters. They could never be show dogs like the Shih Tzu. But they are treasures just the same. Their bright eyes look for their owners to come home from school. They like to run and play with their owners. Do you own a treasure like this?

The Fire Keeper
The Fire

The smoke from the fire curled around Little Fox's head. He choked and fanned it away. "Just once I wish I could go on the hunt with the men," he said.

White Cloud, his mother, looked up from her bed of animal skins. She smiled at the small boy crouched over the fire.

"Who would take care of me then, Little Fox?" she asked. "Who would keep the fire going?"

Little Fox smiled back at her. He poked at the fire to make the orange flames burn more brightly. "I will, Mother. But soon you will be well. Then you will not need me to take care of you."

White Cloud moved her hurt leg under the skins. Little Fox looked up as she moaned.

"I should have gone with you to the spring. I would have killed that wild pig! Then he would not have hurt you."

He grabbed a spear from the wall and thrust toward a shadow.

"There! He is dead!" Little Fox pretended. He leaned the spear against the wall.

White Cloud laughed at the boy. Little Fox was glad to hear her laughter for he knew how much she suffered. She could not stand on her leg. So Shining Star, his older sister, had gone to get water from the spring.

Little Fox sighed and picked up a small stone. The men had gone on the hunt two days ago. Little Fox wanted to go hunting, but the men all thought he was too little. All he could do was take care of the fire. He felt the end of the stone. It was sharp enough. Little Fox began to scratch on the wall of the cave with the sharp stone. He moved the stone back and forth.

White Cloud saw the four legs of a buffalo appear. Then came its back. Soon its head looked down from the wall. How Little Fox could draw!

"Soon he will be old enough to go on the fall hunt with the men," she thought. "He will hunt the animals he draws so well." She closed her eyes and lay back on the bed.

Little Fox mixed the red clay with water. He picked up a brush. He had made it himself using fur and a stick. Carefully he painted the buffalo red.

The fire flickered as he dug out burnt sticks to mix with water and make black paint. "I'll add more branches to the fire soon," he said to himself, "but I'll finish my buffalo first."

He frowned at the stone bowl. There was not a drop of water left. "What is taking Shining Star so long?" he thought. "She should be back with the water."

He walked to the mouth of the cave. All he could see were the treetops far below. Little Fox turned back to his painting.

"There is no water to make paint," he thought to himself. "I'll draw with the burned tips of the sticks." He rubbed the sticks over the buffalo. He worked slowly. He added a little black here. He rubbed some out there. Then he stepped back to look.

"There! It is done!" he said to himself. "Now it looks more like a real buffalo."

Mountain Lion

"Little Fox!"

Little Fox dropped the burnt stick and ran to the mouth of the cave. Shining Star scrambled up the last few feet. She stumbled past her brother.

"Mountain lion!" Shining Star cried. She pointed down the side of the cliff. Little Fox could see the mountain lion leaping from rock to rock.

"What is it?" called her mother, trying to sit up. Shining Star ran to her side. "A mountain lion!" she cried.

"Use the fire to scare him away!" White Cloud called to Little Fox.

Little Fox reached for one of the burning branches to frighten the mountain lion. But the fire had gone out!

The mountain lion leaped across the rocks. It landed in the mouth of the cave. There it crouched, snarling!

Little Fox felt for the spear leaning against the cave wall. His fingers closed around the spear. His mouth was dry. This was no game. The mountain lion was no shadow to kill!

Little Fox yelled as loudly as he could. He ran at the mountain lion and threw the spear. Surprised, the mountain lion stepped back. It lost its footing and slid down a few feet. The spear flew over its head. Then Little Fox heard shouts below. The hunters were home!

The mountain lion turned quickly. It leaped from the rocks and was gone. Little Fox stood still as his father climbed into the cave.

"I let the fire go out, Father." Little Fox hung his head. "I didn't think keeping a fire was as important as hunting."

His father stooped down. "You were wrong to let the fire go out, Little Fox. You are the fire keeper. What would we do without our fire? It warms us and protects us." He looked at the boy's bent head.

"But you were brave today, Little Fox. You will be a good hunter when you are a little older."

Little Fox lifted his head and his eyes brightened. "You forgive me?" he whispered.

"Yes, but you must be the fire keeper until the hunt is over," his father replied.

"Oh, I will, Father!" Little Fox cried. "I'll keep the fire burning!" He ran to tend the fire. Soon Little Fox had the fire burning brightly.

That night Little Fox mixed his paints carefully. Before long a mountain lion glared down from the cave wall. Its yellow eyes glowed in the light of the fire. From then on, when Little Fox looked at the mountain lion, he remembered to tend the fire!

The Liberty Bell

A New Bell

The assembly men walked into the new statehouse. The paint on the walls smelled new. The tables were polished. The men were pleased with their new meeting house.

"Our meeting house is done," one man said. "Now all we need is a special bell to call people to the meetings."

Because no one in America made bells, the men sent a letter to England. They ordered a two-thousand-pound bell. They asked for these words from Leviticus 25:10 to be written on it:

Proclaim liberty throughout the land
to all the inhabitants thereof.

Late in the summer the huge bell arrived. While workmen hauled the bell to the statehouse lawn, carpenters hammered some wooden beams together. Then they hung the bell on the wooden beams for everyone to see.

Clang, clang, it rang. Then—clunk. A crack ran up one side. The new bell was broken.

The workmen took the bell down. Two men said they would try to fix it. They had never made a bell before, but they melted it and molded it.

When the men finished, everyone came to listen to it ring.

Clank, clank! The people held their ears. That sound would not do. The two men had to melt the bell and mold it once more.

At last the bell was hung in the tower of the statehouse.

Liberty

In 1775 the war for America's freedom started. The British troops came closer and closer to the statehouse. All the bells were moved to another city. They would be safe there.

Carefully the men hid the bell under a church. It lay in darkness a long time. At last the British left. The bell went back to the statehouse.

Soon America was free! Excitement filled the air. In the statehouse tower the bell rang long and loud. "We Americans are free from British rule," it seemed to say. "Liberty!"

For nearly sixty years the bell rang for every meeting. But it had begun to crack. Then one day a loud clank came from the tower. The crack ran up one side of the bell. The bell would ring no more.

Years later workmen were repairing and cleaning the statehouse. The men took the bell from the steeple and placed it on a stand. People came from far and near to see the bell. They thought about their freedom when they looked at the bell. They began to call it the "Liberty Bell."

The bell has not rung since those days long ago. But even today Americans visit it in Philadelphia, where it hangs on a stand. They still seem to hear it ringing, "America is free! Liberty!"

Bridges

Boats sail on the rivers,
　　And ships sail on the seas;
But clouds that sail across the sky
　　Are prettier far than these.

There are bridges on the rivers,
　　As pretty as you please;
But the bow that bridges heaven,
　　And overtops the trees,
And builds a road from earth to sky,
　　Is prettier far than these.

by Christina Rossetti

Gifts from the Wise Men

(taken from Matthew 2:1-12)

A New Star

"Look! Look up in the sky! This is the brightest, most glorious star I have ever seen."

A wise man stood outside pointing to the sky and calling to his friends. Other wise men came hurrying out. Their eyes grew wide as they looked at the marvelous star.

"This is wonderful!" one friend said. "I have studied the sky for many years, but I have never seen anything like this. This star is in the sky for a special reason."

"It means that the King is born," another wise man said. The other men nodded when they heard these words. This was something they had read about and had waited for. "We must leave right away and go to the country where the star leads us," one said. "We will find the new King there."

"We do not know how long we will have to travel or how far we will have to go," said one of the men. "We will need many camels to carry our food and water. I will tell the servants what to pack."

As the servants packed the things needed for the trip, the wise men talked with each other.

"We will be seeing a very special King," said one. "We cannot go empty-handed."

"We must take Him our most precious gifts," agreed another. "But what will we take?"

All the wise men thought and thought, trying to decide what would be best to take to this special King.

"Everything is done," said the servants. "The camels are ready to go. We have packed plenty of food and warm blankets."

The wise men shook their heads. "But we do not have everything we need."

The servants were eager to help. "Is there anything else we can get for you?"

"No," came the reply. "There are some things that *we* must get. We must choose our best gifts to take to the new King."

The servants held the camels as the wise men walked slowly back inside.

"What treasures can we take?" the wise men wondered. "What can we take that would be good enough for this wonderful King?"

Treasures for the King

When the wise men came back outside, one was carrying something heavy. It was wrapped in a soft velvet cloth.

"Look!" he said to his friends. "I am going to take the new King a gift of gold."

"That is a generous gift," another agreed. "I am going to give the new King a gift of frankincense." He opened a little carved box. A fragrant smell drifted on the evening breeze.

"Your gifts are thoughtful ones," said another wise man. "I, too, have a gift." He held out a fine white bottle. As he opened the bottle, the sweet smell of myrrh filled the air.

"The King will be pleased with your gifts," said one of the servants. "But the trip will be a long and dangerous one. Robbers hide along the roadside to attack rich caravans such as yours. We will have to be alert at all times."

"Yes, you are right," said one man. "If they steal our food or other things, it will be bad, but at any cost we must keep them from stealing our gifts for the King."

The other men nodded. They knew that the gifts they were taking to the new King would be the most important things they carried.

Carefully the servants placed the precious gifts into the bags loaded on the camels' backs.

"Now we have everything we need," they said. "We are ready to leave."

Once again the servants held the camels
and the wise men climbed on. Then the wise
men and servants rode toward Jerusalem.
264

Night after night the big brown camels
plodded over the dreary desert. Sometimes
the wise men rested or slept. But one of
the servants would always stay awake to
keep the treasures safe.

265

A Wicked Plan

When the small caravan reached Jerusalem, people stopped to look at it.

"What is that?" they whispered to each other.

"Important men who have come from a far land," others whispered back. "Why are they here?" But the children were not afraid. They ran alongside the camels to lead the wise men to the palace. There the wise men went in to see King Herod.

"Where is the new King of the Jews?" they asked Herod. "We have seen His star in the east and are come to worship Him. We know that He was born, but we cannot find Him. Can you tell us where He lives?"

King Herod did not reply right away. He began to walk back and forth. "If this new King is so famous, why have I not heard about Him?" he thought. "Will the people begin to follow Him instead of me?"

266

Then Herod turned to the wise men. "I will ask my chief priests and scribes where the new King was born."

Herod's scribes gathered to look in the temple scrolls. "We read here that the new King will be born in Bethlehem," they told Herod and the wise men.

The angry king left the room. "I should have heard about this new King!" he shouted. "Is He really more important than I am?" Herod's eyes grew dark. "I am afraid of this King. I do not want the people to worship Him when they should be worshiping me. I will not let them do it!"

Then the evil king thought up a wicked plan. He laughed and rubbed his hands together. Then he came back to the wise men and smiled at them. "Go to Bethlehem and find the child," he said. "Then come tell me where He is. I want to worship Him too."

The wise men did not know that Herod really planned to kill the new King. They bowed low before the king and went out. Leaving the palace, they headed toward Bethlehem, following the bright star.

Precious Treasure

The camels plodded through the quiet streets of Bethlehem. The tired men rode silently, following the moving star.

"Look!" called the first man when they had gone a little farther. "The star has stopped over that house."

The wise men knew they had reached the end of their long trip. They rejoiced with new strength and energy. "We have found the place. Let us go in and worship the King!"

When they entered the house, they saw Mary and a young child.

"Is this child the new King?" they asked.

"Yes, He is," replied Mary. "And His name is Jesus."

The wise men bowed low before Jesus.

"We have precious things to offer the King," they said. "We have

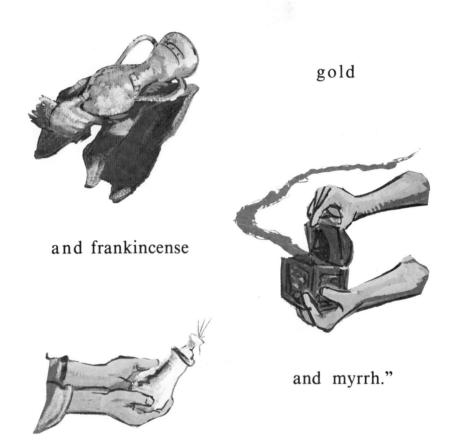

gold

and frankincense

and myrrh."

Silently they placed their gifts before the young child. Silently they worshiped Him.

As the wise men rose to leave, Mary and Joseph thanked them for the gifts.

The wise men bowed again. "We wanted to bring our most precious treasures to give to the King."

270

The wise men led their camels through the streets of Bethlehem. At the city gates, the men climbed onto their beasts. They turned the camels toward their own country.

"We must go back to Herod," one wise man said suddenly. "Remember, he wants to worship the new King too."

So the caravan turned around to travel back to Jerusalem. But that night all the men had a dream. The next morning one said, "I dreamed something last night that troubles me. I dreamed that God told me not to go back to Herod. In my dream God told me that Herod is a wicked man. He wants to kill the new King."

"I had the same dream!" exclaimed another.

"I did too!" said a third.

"God must have told us this so that Jesus would be kept safe," they all agreed. "We must go back home another way."

The wise men turned their caravan away from Jerusalem. As they rode through the desert, they praised God for sending His Son.

"I am glad we gave our gifts to Jesus," said one wise man, "for Jesus is God's special gift to us."

"We gave our best," the others agreed. "But it was so little compared to God's gift—the very best treasure of all!"

Mr. Squirrel's Treasure

I Want a Treasure

The sun shone brightly in the forest. Mr. Beaver felt the cool crisp breeze blowing through his windows. He hummed a happy tune as he wrapped a scarf around his neck. Off he went to visit his good friend, Mr. Squirrel.

Rap! Rap! Rap! Mr. Beaver's tail knocked sharply against the wall. A gloomy voice called, "Come in." When Mr. Beaver went in, he saw Mr. Squirrel sitting at the table with his chin in his hands.

279

"Why are you sad, Mr. Squirrel?" asked Mr. Beaver.

Mr. Squirrel stood up and walked slowly across the room. "I want to find a precious treasure," he said. "I won't be happy until I have a treasure as good as the ones in this book." He held up a large book with many pictures.

Mr. Beaver looked carefully at the book. There were chests filled with gold and silver. There were rings and bracelets of diamonds. There were treasures of all kinds.

Mr. Beaver scratched his head. "How can you get a treasure?" he asked. "No one in the forest has enough money for such grand things."

274

"I don't know." Mr. Squirrel sat down again with his chin in his hands. He thought and thought. Suddenly his face lit up. He clapped his hands and laughed in excitement. "I'll visit Wise Old Owl. He knows everything! He will tell me where I can find my treasure. Will you come with me?"

Mr. Beaver nodded. "I will come because I am your friend."

The two friends hurried outside. White clouds sailed across the blue sky. Mr. Beaver twitched his nose and thumped his flat tail on the ground several times. He was happy just to be alive on such a nice day.

But Mr. Squirrel did not think about the blue sky or the white clouds. All he could think about was his treasure. In fact, he thought about it so hard that he did not look where he was going. At the edge of the brook, Mr. Squirrel's foot slipped on a wet stone. With a splash he fell into the cold water.

"Help me! Help me!" He waved his arms wildly as he called. "I can't swim. Please pull me out!"

Mr. Beaver hurried to the brook and jumped in. In no time at all he had pulled Mr. Squirrel to the other side of the brook.

Mr. Squirrel shivered and shook from head to foot. "I'm cold and wet," he said. "But thank you for pulling me out of the water. You are a good friend."

Look in the Pond

At last the two friends stood underneath Owl's tree and looked up. Wise Old Owl stared back at them, not moving or even blinking his eyes.

Mr. Squirrel twisted his paws together and scuffed his toe in the dirt. Wise Old Owl looked so stern! At last Mr. Squirrel cleared his throat and began.

"Wise Old Owl," Mr. Squirrel said, "I want to find a precious treasure. I want to be rich. You know so much, and you are a wise owl. Will you tell me where I can find a special treasure?"

Owl's eyes blinked once. "Look in the pond," he said. That was all. He ruffled his feathers, and then he closed his eyes.

When Mr. Squirrel heard these words, his little ears twitched and his eyes became bright. "In the pond! In the pond!" he said. "We can't waste a moment, Mr. Beaver! There must be gold in the pond!"

Mr. Squirrel started running toward the pond. Mr. Beaver was not so fast. He had a hard time keeping up with Mr. Squirrel. But once again, Mr. Squirrel did not look where he was going. He caught his foot between two tree roots.

"Help me, please Mr. Beaver!" Mr. Squirrel's arms waved wildly in the air. Mr. Beaver ran to his friend. He pulled this way and that trying to get him loose. But he could not. Mr. Squirrel was stuck.

"Stand still," Mr. Beaver told his friend. "I will chew the roots in two."

He chewed and chewed the big roots. At last Mr. Squirrel pulled his foot free.

"Thank you!" said Mr. Squirrel gratefully. "You are a good friend."

The Rock in the Pond

Mr. Beaver and Mr. Squirrel walked the rest of the way to the pond. They stood at the edge and looked in. The water was as smooth and as clear as glass.

"All I can see is you and me," Mr. Squirrel said with surprise. "Maybe there is something on the bottom of the pond that we should see. Will you go down and look?"

"Yes, I'll look," said Mr. Beaver, and he jumped into the cold water.

In a few moments Mr. Beaver's head popped back up. His teeth held a bright rock. Many different colors sparkled in the sunlight.

Mr. Beaver carefully laid the rock in front of his friend. "Maybe this is your treasure," he said.

"Yes, this must be it," Mr. Squirrel said eagerly. He grabbed the rock and turned it this way and that. He quivered all over with happiness. "Now we can go home."

That night Mr. Squirrel put the rock next to his pillow. He dreamed of all the things he would be able to do with his new treasure.

The sun rose bright and red the next morning. Mr. Squirrel sat up and stretched. Then he quickly reached for his rock.

It wasn't bright and sparkling anymore! It was dry and dark and ugly. "This rock isn't a real treasure after all," Mr. Squirrel cried. "When it's dry, it doesn't even sparkle."

He hurried over to Mr. Beaver's house and went in without knocking. "You must come with me back to Owl's tree," he said. "I have to speak to him again."

Through the woods and over the brook the two friends hurried together. When they reached Owl's tree, they found him staring straight at them. He was not moving a feather or blinking an eye.

Mr. Squirrel stood nervously on one foot. Then he stood on the other. "Wise Old Owl," he said, "you told me to look in the pond for my treasure, and I did. I found a rock that I thought was my treasure, but it was not a real treasure. Today it is dry and dark and ugly. What should I do now?"

Owl's head moved a little and his eyes blinked twice. "Look in the pond," he repeated. He would not say another word. His feathers ruffled a little, and he closed his eyes.

284

Finding the Treasure

"Look in the pond. Look in the pond." Mr. Squirrel muttered as he walked away.

Mr. Beaver ran after him. "Maybe there is still a treasure there that we missed," he said.

"You may be right," Mr. Squirrel's face brightened. "At least we could look." So the two friends hurried back to the pond.

Together they tiptoed up to the pond and stood at the edge looking in. The water was as smooth and as clear as glass.

"All I can see is you and me," said Mr. Squirrel sadly. "I think Owl must be wrong."

285

"But maybe we are supposed to wait," said Mr. Beaver. "Maybe the treasure will come to you."

So the two friends sat down on the ground. They stared into the water and waited.

As Mr. Squirrel stared into the water at himself and his good friend, he began to remember all the things Mr. Beaver had done. He remembered how Mr. Beaver had come on this treasure hunt without grumbling. He remembered how Mr. Beaver had saved him from drowning in the brook. He remembered how Mr. Beaver had freed him from the tree roots when he was stuck. He remembered how Mr. Beaver had dived into the cold water of the pond to look for the treasure for him.

"What a good friend Mr. Beaver is," he thought to himself.

Suddenly Mr. Squirrel jumped up from the ground and hopped around and around. His tail twitched and his whiskers wiggled. "I have found it!" he cried. "I have found my treasure!" He pulled Mr. Beaver up from the ground and twirled around with him.

"Owl was right," cried Mr. Squirrel. "I looked and looked into the pond, and I found my precious treasure. See!" He pulled Mr. Beaver over to the edge of the pond. "Look in the water. You are my treasure! I must thank Owl."

Mr. Beaver was happy that he was a treasure, but he asked, "Does that mean you won't be rich?"

"Oh, but I am very rich!" replied Mr. Squirrel. "Anyone is rich enough who has a friend as faithful as you. Come back home with me. We will have some tea."

"I would be glad to." Mr. Beaver's face glowed. Together the two friends walked arm in arm back through the forest.

GLOSSARY

This glossary has information about selected words found in this reader. You can find meanings of words as they are used in the stories. Certain unusual words such as foreign names are included so you can pronounce them correctly when you read.

The pronunciation symbols below show how to pronounce each vowel and several of the less familiar consonants.

ă	pat	ĕ	pet	î	fierce
ā	pay	ē	be	ŏ	pot
â	care	ĭ	pit	ō	go
ä	father	ī	pie	ô	paw, for

oi	oil	ŭ	cut	zh	vision
ŏŏ	book	û	fur	ə	ago, item,
ōō	boot	*th*	the		pencil, atom,
yōō	abuse	th	thin		circus
ou	out	hw	which	ər	butter

a·bil·i·ty | ə **bĭl'** ĭ tē | The power or skill to do something.

ad·vice | ăd **vīs'** | Opinion about what to do; guidance.

age | āj | The amount of time a person has lived.

a·lert | ə **lûrt'** | Quick to notice or understand.

an·swer | **ăn'** sər | or | **än'** sər | To speak or write in reply to something said or written.

a·part·ment | ə **pärt'** mənt | A room or set of rooms for one household. An apartment is in a building or house that usually has other rooms or sets of rooms like it.

Aus·tra·lia | ô **strāl'** yə | A continent southeast of Asia between the Pacific and Indian oceans.

ba·boon | bă **boon'** | A large African monkey with a long, narrow face.

barbed wire | bärbd' wīr' | Twisted strands of wire having sharp hooks or barbs at regular intervals. Barbed wire is used in fences.

bark¹ | bärk | The short gruff sound made by a dog.

bark² | bärk | The outer covering of the trunks, branches, and roots of trees. Bark can be thick and rough or thin and smooth.

bleat | blēt | To utter the cry of a sheep.

broad | brôd | Large from side to side; wide.

baboon

barbed wire

290

buf·fa·lo | bŭf′ ə lō′ | An animal; the bison of North America. It has a dark brown mane and curved horns.

bug·gy | bŭg′ ē | A small, light carriage pulled by a horse.

cap·tain | kăp′ tən | The leader of a group.

car·a·van | kăr′ ə văn′ | A group of people, animals, or vehicles traveling together, usually in a long line.

cedar

ce·dar | sē′ dər | An evergreen tree with reddish wood that has a pleasant smell. Cedars are related to pines and firs.

chat·ter | chăt′ ər | To make quick, rattling noises.

chick·a·dee | chĭk′ ə dē′ | A small, plump bird with gray, black, and white feathers. It has a call that sounds like its name.

cliff

choc·o·late | chô′ kə lĭt | or | chŏk′ ə lĭt | or | chôk′ lĭt | or | chŏk′ lĭt | A beverage made from roasted and ground cacao beans.

chore | chôr | or | chōr | A small job, usually done on a regular schedule.

Chris·tian | krĭs′ chən | One who has accepted Jesus Christ as Saviour.

ci·der | sī′ dər | The juice that is made from apples that have been ground up and pressed. Cider is used as a drink.

clev·er | klĕv′ ər | Having a quick mind; smart; bright.

cliff | klĭf | A high, steep, or overhanging face of earth or rock.

clump | klŭmp | A thick group of trees or bushes.

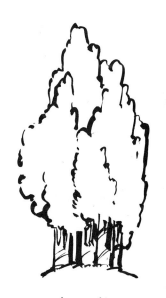

a **clump** of trees

cock | kŏk | To tilt or turn up to one side.

291

comb

corncrib

coil | koil | To wind around a number of times.

comb | kōm | A bright-red strip of flesh on the head of a rooster.

com·pare | kəm pâr' | To say that something is similar.

con·tent | kən tĕnt' | Pleased with what one has or is; satisfied.

coop | kōop | A cage or pen for chickens.

corn·crib | kôrn' krĭb' | A structure for storing and drying ears of corn.

croc·o·dile | krŏk' ə dīl' | A large reptile with thick skin, sharp teeth, and long, narrow jaws. Crocodiles live in wet places throughout the tropics. Alligators and crocodiles look very much alike, but crocodiles have narrower jaws.

crouch | krouch | To bend low; stoop; squat.

den | dĕn | The home or shelter of a wild animal.

de·sire | dĭ zīr' | To wish or long for; want.

dodge | dŏj | To avoid by moving quickly out of the way.

dog bis·cuit | dôg bĭs' kĭt | or | dŏg bĭs' kĭt | A hard, dry food product made for dogs.

dread·ed | drĕd' ĭd | Greatly feared.

ea·ger | ē' gər | Wanting something very much; full of desire.

el·e·phant | ĕl' ə fənt | A very large animal of Africa or Asia; it has long tusks and a long trunk.

em·per·or | ĕm' pər ər | A man who rules an empire.

292

en·vy | ĕn′ vē | A feeling of resentment at someone who has something you want; jealousy.

es·cape | ĭ skāp′ | To get free; break loose.

eu·ca·lyp·tus | yōō′ kə lyp′ təs | A tall tree that grows in Australia and other warm regions. An oil with a strong smell is made from its leaves. Its wood is used for building.

ex·claim | ik sklām′ | To speak out suddenly and loudly, as from surprise.

faint | fānt | Not clearly heard, weak: *a faint cry*.

fair | fâr | A large public display of farm products.

fa·vor·ite | fā′ vər ĭt | Liked best.

flock | flŏk | A group of one kind of animal that lives, travels, or feeds together.

fly ball | flī bôl | A baseball hit high into the air, usually into the outfield.

fold¹ | fōld | To bend over or double up so that one part lies on another.

fold² | fōld | An area that is closed in, used to keep sheep.

frank·in·cense | frăngk′ ĭn sĕns′ | A sweet-smelling incense.

gears | gîrz | Wheels with teeth around the edges that fit into the teeth of other wheels. Gears are used to send motion or power from one machine part to another.

gem | jĕm | A precious stone that has been cut and polished to be used as a jewel.

gen·er·ous | jĕn′ ər əs | Unselfish.

glare | glâr | To stare angrily.

eucalyptus

fold

glider

gourd

knapsack

gleam | glēm | A bright beam or flash of light.

glid·er | glī′ dər | A special airplane without an engine.

gloom·y | gloō′ mē | Discouraged; sad.

glo·ri·ous | glôr′ ē əs | or | glōr′ ē əs | Magnificent.

glow | glō | To give off a steady light; shine.

gourd | gôrd | or | gōrd | or | goōrd | A hard, dry, hollow shell of a fruit related to the pumpkin and squash.

grum·ble | grŭm′ bəl | To complain in a low, discontented voice; mutter discontentedly.

heart | härt | The organ that pumps blood throughout the body.

hea·then | hē′ then | Persons who do not believe in God.

hood·ed | hoōd′ ĭd | Covered, as if with a hood.

in·hab·i·tant | ĭn hăb′ ĭ tənt | A person who lives in a particular place.

in·vis·i·ble | ĭn vĭz′ ə bəl | Not capable of being seen.

kan·ga·roo | kăng gə roō′ | An animal of Australia with long, strong hind legs and a long tail. The female carries her newborn young in a pouch on the outside of her body.

keen | kēn | Very quick or sensitive: *a keen sense of smell.*

knap·sack | năp′ săk′ | A canvas or leather bag made to be worn on the back. A knapsack is used to carry supplies on a hike.

ko·a·la | kō ä′ lə | An animal of Australia that looks something like a small, furry teddy bear. It lives in eucalyptus trees and feeds on their leaves.

lamb | lăm | A young sheep.

learn | lûrn | To gain knowledge through study or experience.

lib·er·ty | lĭb′ ər tē | Freedom from the control or rule of another.

lo·cust | lō′ kəst | A kind of grasshopper.

locust

lum·ber | lŭm′ bər | To move or walk in a clumsy and often noisy way.

med·al | mĕd′ l | A flat, round piece of metal with a design or writing on it. Medals are awarded to honor outstanding achievements.

meek | mēk | Gentle, kind, and patient; humble.

mil·ler | mĭl′ ər | One who works in or owns a mill for grinding grain.

medal

mis·sion·ar·y | mĭsh′ ə nĕr′ ē | A person sent out to spread the gospel of salvation to the world.

moan·ings | mōn ĭngs | Long, low sounds of pain or sadness.

mo·tor | mō′ tər | A device or machine that provides the power to make something go; engine.

mouth | mouth | 1. The part of the body through which a person or animal takes in food. 2. An opening.

motor

mut·ter | mŭt′ ər | To speak or say in a low voice that is not clear; mumble.

myrrh | mûr | A sweet-smelling perfume of the Far East, used as incense.

nar·ra·tor | năr′ āt′ ər | One who tells a story.

nip | nĭp | To give a small, sharp bite or bites to.

palace

porcupine

a kangaroo's **pouch**

pack | păk | A group of similar animals.

pal·ace | păl′ ĭs | The official residence of a king, queen, or other ruler.

ped·dler | pĕd′ lər | A person who travels from place to place selling goods.

perch | pûrch | To land or rest on.

pitch·er¹ | pĭch′ ər | The baseball player who throws the ball to the batter.

pitch·er² | pĭch′ ər | A container used to hold and pour out liquids. A pitcher has a handle on one side and a spout on the other.

plank | plăngk | A thick, wide, long piece of wood that has been sawed.

plod | plŏd | To walk heavily or with great effort.

por·cu·pine | pôr′ kyə pīn′ | An animal covered with long, sharp spines called quills.

por·ridge | pôr ĭj | or | pŏr′ ĭj | A thick soup made by boiling oatmeal or another grain in water or milk.

post | pōst | A straight piece of wood set up in the ground to hold something up.

pouch | pouch | A part of an animal's body that is like a bag or a pocket.

pre·cious | prĕsh′ əs | Of high price or value.

pro·claim | prō klām′ | To announce officially and publicly.

pro·pel·ler | prə pĕl′ ər | A device that is made up of blades. When the blades spin around, they move the air and produce force to propel or move an aircraft.

Pu·tu por·ridge | po͞o′ to͞o pôr′ ĭj | or | po͞o′ to͞o pŏr′ ĭj | An African soup made by boiling grains in water.

py·thon | **pī′** thŏn | A very large, nonpoisonous snake of Africa, Asia, and Australia. Pythons coil around and crush the animals they eat.

quill | kwĭl | One of the sharp, hollow spines of a porcupine.

quiv·er | **kwĭv** ər | To shake with a slight vibrating motion.

quill

ranch | rănch | A large farm on which cattle, sheep, or horses are raised.

re·triev·er | rĭ **trē′** vər | A kind of dog that can be trained to find and bring back birds or animals that have been shot.

ruf·fle | **rŭf′** əl | To disturb the smooth appearance of.

sag | săg | To sink or hang down.

scam·per | **skăm′** pər | To run quickly.

scribe | skrīb | A person who copied books, letters, and other kinds of written material before printing was invented.

scroll | skrōl | A roll of paper, parchment, or other material that has writing on it. Each end is rolled around a rod or cylinder.

scroll

scuff | skŭf | To scrape or drag the feet in walking.

sense | sĕns | To become aware of.

shed | shĕd | To lose in a natural way; drop.

shell | shĕl | To remove the outer covering from.

shep·herd | **shĕp′** ərd | A person who takes care of a flock of sheep.

Shih Tzu | shēd **zōō′** | A small, alert dog, originally from China.

shoe | shōō | Outer covering for the foot.

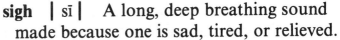

sigh | sī | A long, deep breathing sound made because one is sad, tired, or relieved.

sign | sīn | An event or action that is believed to be proof that something will happen.

sim·mer | sĭm′ ər | To cook below or just at the boiling point.

sleek | slēk | Smooth and shiny.

slith·er | slĭth′ ər | To move along by gliding, as a snake.

snarl | snärl | To growl, especially while showing teeth.

snatch | snăch | To grab suddenly and quickly.

snug | snŭg | Pleasant and comfortable; cozy.

snug·gle | snŭg′ əl | To press close; nestle.

son | sŭn | A male child.

soup | sōop | A liquid food prepared by boiling meat and / or vegetables in water.

spark·le | spär′ kəl | To give off sparks of light; glitter.

spe·cial | spĕsh′ əl | Different from what is usual or common; exceptional.

speck·led | spĕk əld | Dotted with small spots.

spring | sprĭng | A natural fountain or flow of water.

staff | stăf | or | stäf | A long stick with a hook at one end used by a shepherd.

stalk | stôk | To walk in a stiff manner.

stall | stôl | An enclosed space for one animal in a barn or stable.

stam·pede | stăm **pēd′** | A sudden, violent rush of startled or scared animals.

snarl

a **speckled** egg

298

steep | stēp | Having a sharp slope.

stee·ple | stē′ pəl | A tall tower rising from the roof of a building.

stern | stûrn | Grave and severe; strict.

stray | strā | Wandering; lost.

street·car | strēt′ kär′ | A car that runs on rails and carries passengers along a regular route through city streets.

a **steep** hill

sway | swā | To move from side to side.

tab·er·na·cle | tăb′ ər năk′ əl | A temple or place of worship.

tar | tär | A thick, sticky, dark substance that is used to pave roads and cover roofs.

tas·sel | tăs′ əl | A bunch of loose threads on cords that are tied together at one end and hanging free at the other.

streetcar

taste | tāst | To notice the flavor of by taking into the mouth.

throne | thrōn | The chair where a king, queen, or other ruler sits.

thrust | thrŭst | To push with force; shove.

thun·der | thŭn′ dər | To produce sounds like the rumbling or crashing noise that accompanies a bolt of lightning.

tongue | tŭng | The piece of flesh in the mouth, used in tasting, chewing, and swallowing food.

tract | trăkt | A leaflet or pamphlet presenting the plan of salvation, Bible doctrines, or some other subject.

troop | tro͞op | A group of soldiers.

trot | trŏt | To run quickly.

tassel

trudge | trŭj | To walk slowly with effort, as if one is tired or carrying a heavy burden.

wolf

zebra

twitch | twĭch | To move with a quick jerk.

val·ley | văl′ ē | A long, narrow area of low land between mountains or hills.

vel·vet | věl′ vĭt | A soft, smooth cloth with a short, thick, plush surface.

wolf | wo͝olf | An animal that lives mostly in northern regions and feeds on the flesh of other animals.

wor·ship | wûr′ shĭp | To love and obey God from the heart.

yelp | yĕlp | To utter a sharp, short bark or cry.

ze·bra | zē′ brə | An African animal that is related to the horse. Its body is marked with black and whitish stripes.